TODDLER DISCIPLINE 101

CHRISTINA JAMES

To my husband, my partner, and my friend,
your unwavering love and support are the
cornerstones of my journey. Thank you for your
believing in me and making me a better mother.

To my children, thank you for the laughter
and challenges. You are my inspiration.

To you my reader, remember you are not alone in
your journey. It takes a village, welcome to ours.

TABLE OF CONTENTS

INTRODUCTION

Mayhem and Madness

Toddlers are insane, and they will drive you crazy, too. Having a toddler in your household can feel like living in a deranged circus run by an emotionally unstable little person. And you, the circus owner, are running yourself ragged from dawn till dusk, putting out fires and attempting to establish some kind of order to this nonsensical chaos.

But running around after your little one is not your only challenge. Oh no, most definitely not. Not only are you trying to keep up with them physically, but you're also attempting to manage them emotionally. A toddler's mood might change dramatically at any given moment. You'll find yourself dumbfounded when your cute little baby suddenly transforms into a tantrum-throwing toddler who falls on the floor wailing and kicking because you sliced their sandwich in the "incorrect" shape or gave them the wrong-colored cup. There is no use in trying to keep up with their onslaught of feelings because even as you try to handle one, the next one is already gearing up to drown you in its waves.

However, amidst all that chaos, there are windows of fun, laughter, and pure joy that show you that all your hard work and suffering is not for nothing. Seeing a child on the cusp between infancy and toddlerhood reminds us of life's beauty, our lost curiosity for the basic things, and the importance of good habits and consistency.

But in all reality, will your child ever be cuter than this? Your 2-year-old Tweedledee is giddy, silly, and enjoying life carefree. And beyond the cuteness, your little one's love for you is immense and passionate at this age. You are the center of their universe; they look to you for approval, disapproval, and any other commands or reactions to help guide them. And we as parents are oh-so eager to start teaching our little ones and instructing them on what to do, how to act, what to say, how to behave, what to wear, what habits to form… etc.

It's hard enough to teach them all these skills when they're cooperative, let alone when they've started their rebellion.

It is a common misconception among adults that young children have ears capable of hearing. Does your toddler acknowledge commands like, "Be quiet," "Don't touch that," "Don't eat your boogers," or "Stop pulling mommy's skirt"? Maybe once in a blue moon. They can sure make you wonder if there's something wrong with their hearing. They are, however, perfectly capable of hearing words relating to food. While commands like, "Stay in your bed," might not merit a response from your toddler, she will be able to hear you munching on a snack in the next galaxy over.

At least toddlers can be predictable; they love to make a fool out of you. A toddler will stare blankly at the store owner if you tell her to wave hello. You ask her to say "hi" to Grandma? She'll act like she's never heard of the woman before. If you instruct her to keep breathing, she will hold her breath until she faints.

Depending on your life's course, your 2T may be a darling or a raging madman. Please be aware that these behaviors are a normal part of their cognitive and emotional development regardless of who or what she is.

The tantrums are nothing to be ashamed of or punished for. It's a demand for attention, a plea for sleep, or a rallying cry for stricter, more stable boundaries. Your youngster is pushing and pulling to test his blossoming independence. He is torn between the tremendous desire to overstep his boundaries and the frantic need to know he is being held back.

For first-time parents, it might be pretty confusing. Often, it leads to a lot of regret, guilt, and frustration about your parenting style.

I have been there; and I understand how frustrating and overwhelming it can be.

When I first found out I was pregnant with twins, I was so excited. Twins! How cool is that! I could imagine all the fun family pictures, the cute outfits, the beautiful outings… my life was going to be like a movie.

Fast forward a few months after a grueling labor, the twins were finally born. I can honestly say I remember very little of those early days or months even. While I was busy pumping, eating my extra 1,000 calories to produce enough milk, changing diapers, washing bottles, and trying to get a little sleep, my husband, mother, and mother-in-law enjoyed all the cuddles and fun of having newborn babies in the house.

Don't get me wrong; I needed all the help I could get and was incredibly grateful for all the support. I did, however, wonder where all the fun and happiness promised in those movies were. After all, being a mother can't only be hard work, right?

When the twins were 16 months old, I had my third child. Imagine my surprise when I finally had bonding moments with a newborn baby. It was true bliss. I realized all that I had been missing out on with the twins. To top it all off, the twins were used to sharing their mom and having multiple caretakers, so it did not shift the dynamic much.

My third baby was incredibly quick. She was body crawling by two months, full-on crawling at four months, and walking by seven months. By the time she was 18 months old, she was speaking in complete sentences. My husband called me one day while I was out shopping, laughing hysterically and telling me that he had sneezed, and our little girl looked up at him and said, "God bless you!"

It felt like I had triplets. Three little kids with the same capabilities and going through their terrible twos together. Sigh.

We lived in Minnesota at the time. If you need to know anything about Minnesota, it's that the winters are horrible and can last up to six months at times—definitely not toddler-friendly weather.

Getting three little tots into their warm snow gear, boots, mittens, hats, and scarves can take an entire hour. Only for them to spend 5 minutes outside and come running back inside holding up their little cold pink hands and sobbing about their fingers burning from the cold. After that first outing, they did not want to venture out again.

Needless to say, I was determined to get out of spending the winter in Minnesota. A more patient and adventure-driven mother might be up for the challenge. Not me!

So naturally, when I found out that I was expecting my fourth baby, I told my husband that I was not spending six months out of the year cooped up indoors with four stir-crazy little ones.

When a job opportunity arose in a warmer state, we packed our bags and moved.

My fourth baby was born two weeks after the twins turned three.

Yep, you heard that right. Four children ages three and under.

The twins, Anthony and Izzy, were three years old, followed by my one-and-a-half-year-old Lily and now a newborn baby boy, Jamie. I was now in a new state with no family or help, and to top it all off, my husband was working 60 hours a week. Smart move, moving right…

It was chaos, but I survived, and so will you.

My name is Christina James, and over the years, I've guided many new parents to overcome common parenting challenges, including managing power struggles and tantrums. I've helped them identify the root causes of their parenting problems and solve them. Finally, I've decided to write a book to reach a wider audience. My goal is to make parenting a more enjoyable and fulfilling experience for both parents and their little ones.

If you are kept awake at night by the stress and exhaustion of parenting young children; if you are frustrated by disobedience, disrespect, and tantrums from your toddler; if you worry that you are not doing enough to support your child's development or that you are making mistakes that could have long-lasting consequences, this book is for you.

If you are ready to raise happy, well-adjusted, and successful children and maintain a healthy work-life balance, read on.

CHAPTER 1

What is Positive Parenting?

Proactive Rather Than Reactive Parenting

If you're anything like me, you didn't know much about parenting when you had your first kid. You might have thought raising children can't be rocket science. I mean, they're just tiny little humans. So cute and loving. When you saw out-of-control kids, you thought, "Wow, my kids will never be like that." Ha!

The rebellion started once my older children turned two and a half and my middle child was almost two. There was a nonstop competition of who could make mom tic first. Whining, crying, hitting, and biting appeared to be the go-to whenever the kids were annoyed. And I, in my desperation to get them just to listen, would resort to yelling, chastising, punishing, and spanking. None of which worked.

I felt like a failure.

I had gotten a management degree in college. I consider myself a highly organized person in thought and action, but no amount of organization could have prepared me for this:

How to be a mom.

Not just any mom, though, a happy mom, a devoted mom, a fun mom… a sane mom.

And more importantly, How to raise happy kids.

I was desperate for a solution. I immersed myself in books, podcasts, and programs... anything that could clue me in on raising happy kids without bribing, threatening, or yelling at them.

While there are a lot of resources out there, very few are realistic and could work with my particular situation of having so many little ones. I mean four kids four and under... What are the odds? So, through brainstorming, research, trial, and error, I developed my own system of steps to help with my children's behavioral issues.

This book is a practice-based approach to raising happy toddlers with no yelling, no rewards, and no punishments.

I call it the 3-Step Method.

The best thing about my 3-step method is that it is realistic and achievable. If I can do it, then so can you.

There are three critical steps in each area we address in this book. The first is to identify where your child's behavior stems from, the second is to prevent it in the future, and the third is to address it in the moment.

We have all heard the classic complaint that children should come with an instruction manual. The reality of parenting, however, does not operate that way. Every child is different. My kids all had various meltdowns and tantrums and they also responded differently to each disciplinary tool employed. My friends' and cousins' children differed from mine, and what worked for their families didn't necessarily work for mine. No one set of parenting strategies will be effective for every child in every family and in every situation. And when it comes to positive parenting, there aren't universal guidelines defining what it means to practice it at home. Instead, you can view positive parenting as a lens through which you can make parenting decisions.

Your lens helps you change your perspective on each situation and, therefore, change your reactions and disciplinary tools. For instance, instead of giving your child a smack on the butt or a timeout for painting the wall with your lipstick, you might use this as an opportunity to teach them how to clean up their messes and make amends for damaging mom's property (I'll explain how exactly later).

So, how do we discipline our children?

Discipline comes from the word disciple, which means "Student of a teacher, follower." So, the process of disciplining is, therefore, the process of teaching.

I remember my best teacher in school, Mr N. He taught math. He was a no-nonsense math teacher that never got riled up. He praised when appropriate but, more importantly never mocked, chastised, or berated any of his students. He was consistent with his behavior and style of teaching, and in return, we students were consistently producing good grades. I remember graduating that year with perfect scores on all my math exams. I was so proud of myself.

One year later, I landed with Mrs. B. as a teacher in the same subject. Her style of teaching was the complete opposite. She constantly mocked, yelled, humiliated, and occasionally slapped the back of the heads of her students. She overpraised and compared her students all the time. I failed the subject that year. And I was not the only one either.

All this is to say that the teacher's teaching style affects the child's learning.

Your style of disciplining your child will affect how receptive they are.

Once you can make that shift in outlook regarding the purpose of discipline, you will find yourself shocked at all the new ways you can think of to deal with the issues that arise.

People often confuse positive discipline with no discipline. There is no doubt that discipline is necessary for children.

Lack of discipline is not love; it is neglect.

Positive discipline works on fostering a sense of belonging and significance in the child by following these five beliefs:

1. Create a long-lasting connection with the child (belonging and significance).
2. Create mutual respect with the child and use appropriate encouragement (kind and firm).
3. Looks to be effective long term. (The child is building an identity and learning about the world and how to thrive.)
4. Build social and life skills (respect, problem-solving, identifying emotions, communication, contribution, etc.).
5. Forge confidence (teaches your kid that they are capable, powerful, and autonomous).

In the first seven years of life, children are like sponges. Their brains absorb everything around them, and they are programmed with lifelong skills and, more importantly, lifelong traits. We want our children to grow up and be strong, independent, hardworking, courageous, resilient, fair, kind, etc.

How do we install these traits in them?

As you go through the book, I'll describe multiple situations and examples offering valuable insights and practical strategies. It is my wish that you grasp the understanding of how positive parenting works and envision how it might apply in your household.

To get the most out of this book, I'd encourage you to take notes and jot down ideas that might come to you as you read.

The chapters in this book build on each other. Go in order and implement changes after each chapter.

You may find yourself challenged by some ideas I employ and invite you to embrace. You might think, "oh, that will never work for my kid." If that happens, I recommend you remain open-minded and experiment with those ideas. I may also make some claims in this book that sound hard to believe. I ask you to bear with me and give my ideas a few fair tries. When you see the result, you'll be convinced on your own.

I must warn you that your mindset is the key to your success with these tools. The hardest part of positive discipline is self-discipline for you as a parent. It is tough for a parent to calmly and patiently meet your child's needs if you are not meeting your own needs.

As you read along, if you find implementing these changes too hard for you, I implore you to take a good look in the mirror and figure out what is stopping you from being the parent you deserve to be. More on this later.

To start, I'd like you to think of positive parenting as three zones. There is the yellow zone, where things are sunshine and roses, the orange zone, where problems are brewing; and then there's the red zone, a.k.a. my eardrums are bleeding, or my blood is boiling. Feel free to draw these zones out on paper or download our resources (playful activities, checklists, etc.) online.

Take a few minutes to brainstorm different scenarios or issues you face in each zone.

For example, in my household, yellow would be, playing with trains for Anthony, my oldest. His twin Izzy's yellow would be reading books, and my third Lily's yellow zone activity would be pretend cooking.

Orange would be running over to Mom with a complaint, such as a desired object out of reach. Anything that can quickly be remedied and or turn into a disaster.

And red would be fighting, hitting, destruction of property, and the sorts. Things that turn on the waterworks or the screaming for your kids, and make you lose your cool.

Write a few examples down, and as we go through the book together, think of which tool works best for your situation and try it out.

The parenting tips included in the book will help you to end the meltdowns in your home (come back from the red zone fast), and teach your children how to get back to the yellow zone from orange all by themselves. They will also show you how to enjoy life like a toddler and be present with them in the yellow zone.

CHAPTER 2

Meeting Physical Needs

Little Bodies Talk Loud

By the time your child turns three, their nervous system has progressed significantly, with over 80 percent of it developed. What does this mean?

The toddler years are so crucial in shaping brain development and future well-being. You can set lifelong habits, program your child's brain for success, and install desired values.

My brother was four, and I three, when we moved countries and joined a French school. My mother did not speak French; our only language back then was English. It took us about a week to catch up and be fluent like the other children. A week. Could you imagine learning a new language as an adult? It would take years, let alone a week. My mother still isn't fully fluent 30 years later. But we were toddlers. Toddlers' brains are like a sponge. You can teach them anything.

So, what does your kid need to flourish at this pivotal age? It's pretty simple in theory:
1. A loving and caring connection with you
2. Healthy diet
3. Restful sleep

4. Plenty of mental stimulation through reading and conversing.
5. Plenty of outdoor play
6. Plenty of physical activity
7. A healthy role model

We are no strangers to the challenges that arise while parenting a toddler, particularly when they insist on wearing mismatched shoes or attempt to feed the dog their food, or eat the dog's food.

Even in these unpredictable moments, meeting your child's fundamental needs will do wonders for their growth and development.

Those needs fit into two categories: Physical well-being and emotional well-being.

In this chapter, we'll discuss the physical.

The first step in being happy is making sure that our basic physical needs are met. I know, I know, you might be thinking, "well duh!" And I completely agree - it's simple, common sense and straightforward.

Yet how many of us have skipped breakfast because we just had to get this one thing done first or because we ran out of some crucial ingredient for our favorite breakfast? Fast forward a few hours, and we're a little angry and short-tempered, and we can't quite figure out why.

A simpler and straightforward example might be when you really need to use the bathroom, but your little one just needs one more thing ten times over. You end up holding it an extra 10 or 15 minutes before you finally get to take care of your needs. You'll probably be irritated and, therefore, much more likely to lash out or slip into, as my husband calls it, the knee-jerk reaction parent mode - when you are more likely to scream, yell, and threaten.

Now, you might be thinking, "Wait... I thought we were talking about kids?" and yes, we are. But like any relationship, two components are interacting.

In this case; you and your little one, or if you're like me, ones.

You are the center of this little toddler's world. If you are not doing well, and your needs aren't met, then how could you possibly have a good relationship with your toddler, let alone take care of their needs too?

It's hard enough for us as adults to consistently operate in a sane manner if our basic needs aren't met.

Imagine what it's like for a little human, who's only had a few months' practice at life, and is still figuring out how to talk, identify their emotions and express them.

When I put it like that, it makes total sense that toddlers would be difficult to manage.

So, what are the basic physical needs?

Sleep, eat, bathroom, and health are all necessities for your toddler, just as they are for you; the only difference is that your toddler will need your help to meet those needs.

1. SLEEP

I don't think I need to convince you how hard it is to operate without enough sleep. I'm sure we all have enough experience with sleepless nights and the days that follow those nights. It comes with the territory of being a new mom.

But at least when they're newborns, they're still cute, and don't talk back, hit, or refuse to go to sleep when they're tired. And you might even be able to sneak in a nap while your new baby is sleeping, get some energy, and keep going for the day.

When you have one or more little kids and a newborn, the odds are that your toddler and newborn's naps won't necessarily align and that you won't get a bit more sleep during the day.

Let's troubleshoot:

- A sitter, family member, or friend could stop by and relieve you.
- You could wait for your partner to come home and take a quick nap.
- You can also go to bed earlier. Abandon all chores and projects and take care of your basic needs first.

Problem solved for mom. Now let's talk kids.

Toddlers need a lot of sleep for their health (and behavior), about 11–14 hours daily. During that time, their brain cells create crucial synapses during REM (rapid eye movement) sleep. These pathways make all learning, movement, and cognition possible. They help them make sense of everything they see, hear, taste, touch, and smell as they learn about the world.

When my eldest daughter Izzy turned 3, getting her to nap became a huge battle. She would spend the entire time in her room talking and singing to herself. Since she did this for a few days, we thought she was done napping. However, the tantrums would begin after a couple of days of skipped naps. She could flip between being a happy little girl and a screaming and biting toddler in under a second. I was baffled. My cute little angel biting... what?!

It was almost like she had a multiple personality disorder. One second, she would sweetly ask me for a cup, and the next, she would scream, slam cupboards, and bite furniture because it was not the cup color she wanted.

Her tired signs were very subtle, if nonexistent, too, which made it harder to identify her need for a nap. The solution was easy: make sure she napped or put her to bed at least an hour earlier.

It was a pattern I was seeing with countless mothers and caretakers of 3-year-olds. They think their little one is done napping, but all of a sudden, these crazy tantrums come out of nowhere.

Most toddlers are only done napping once they reach the age of 5 or 6. Potentially sooner if they are consistently getting 12 hours of sleep at night. A friend of mine is a mother to 15 children, and in her house, from 12 p.m. to 2 p.m., everyone under 6 is in their bed. It's how she ensures that they are all in the best shape they can be and, therefore, less likely to have a meltdown.

You can't force anyone to sleep, not even yourself, but with the right environment and consistency, your child will surprise you.

2. EAT

We all know what hangry means. Being angry because you're hungry is not a new concept. Sometimes, we're so busy and wrapped up in what's happening around us that we forget to look inwards and check in with our bodies on what's going on internally until it's too late.

When my husband started working, I was all alone with all three toddlers and a one-month-old newborn baby. I found myself skipping breakfast a lot. It wasn't really by choice.

First, the kids needed to be fed, then the baby wanted to be fed, then the baby wanted to sleep; next the toddlers had to use the bathroom… it never ended. There was always one more thing to take care of before it was finally my turn to sit down and eat.

By the time it got to noon, I'd been awake for at least 6 hours and hadn't eaten a single thing. I was starving, short-tempered, and worried that my milk supply would be affected.

It was genuinely God-sent when my husband came home one day with a meal-in-one powder that he'd gotten from a coworker. I'm no fan of protein shakes. As a very health-conscious eater, I always found something in the ingredients that didn't jive well with me. And even if they passed the ingredient exam, there was the taste factor. None of them tasted good. They all had that fake sweet flavor that I couldn't quite stomach.

"Just try it!" my husband insisted. And so my desperate self did… and holy moly! It was delicious! It's now my quick meal replacer. Just blend it with some berries, almond milk, ice, and maple syrup, and voila! Breakfast is served. Best of all, the kids like to push the blender buttons, so it entertains them. A couple of my kids love it, too, so they get a little bit every day, and it helps me keep them calm while I can get a full breakfast on the table.

But enough about my hunger needs, what about the kids? Have you ever noticed how sometimes, right before dinner, it seems like your kids are falling apart? They're all fighting and whining at you, essentially turning into tiny little terrorists. Or maybe they've just woken up from a nice long nap, and are so crabby.

My oldest daughter, Izzy, was notorious for her hanger tantrums first thing in the morning. When she was two years old, she sometimes woke up between 5 a.m. and 5:30 a.m., which was just too early for me and my husband. She'd go downstairs and happily sit down with a pile of books and read until we were ready to surface. Sounds amazing, right?

The only problem was if we didn't get food in her fast, the tide would quickly turn, and we'd end up with a hysterical, incoherent, sobbing toddler.

One day, my mother-in-law brought over a batch of her banana muffins. She adds collagen in them to make them extra healthy for the kids. The following morning, my husband and I slept in, and there was no screaming. When we finally made it downstairs, we noticed that Izzy had dragged a chair over to the counter, opened the muffin box, and helped herself to a couple of muffins before returning to her books. It was past her breakfast time, and she wasn't screaming.

It was a lightbulb moment. From that day on, we had a series of ready meals and healthy snacks to use in a pinch.

A kid-favorite breakfast in our household is overnight oats, which are incredibly nutritious and made the night before. All you have to do in the morning is take it out of the fridge and scoop it in bowls. It's practically perfect to beat the kid's hunger!

Maybe there's a thing with females and hunger in our family because my younger daughter Lily is the same as her sister. She woke up from her nap one day very, very cranky. I was rushing, trying to get lunch ready.

At one and a half, she could identify her needs and express herself.

She cried, "I'm hungry!" over and over. I told her, "Food is almost ready."

I guess she didn't like that answer because as soon as my back was turned she opened the pantry, took whatever she could get her hands on, and started eating. I turned back to witness her eating some walnuts and shoveling some raw rice into her mouth.

I marveled at her capabilities while feeling embarrassed at my lack of readiness to meet my child's basic needs.

Having a weekly meal plan that includes all the snacks really helps. It eliminates having to think about what to cook in the heat of the moment or revert to handing your child something completely unhealthy just because they're hungry and you're not ready.

I also want to point out that dehydration can sometimes be the real culprit of fatigue, low energy, and bad moods. A glass of water is an excellent quick fix.

Your child must be adequately nourished to dedicate their energy to learning and developing. You don't have to turn every mealtime into a war, but it's important to set positive examples by offering a range of foods and eating together as a family.

Think of your toddler's nutritional needs over the course of a week rather than worrying too much if it appears like they're just eating carbs one day. Because toddlers tend to be picky eaters, mealtimes can be stressful. And you really can't force them to eat - no matter how much you'd like to.

Here are some quick tips to overcome mealtime challenges:

- Story meal time - "Have you ever heard the story of the green bean and the potato?" Leave them on a cliffhanger and ask them to take a bite for the story to continue.
- Animate the object - "Ohh, I'm the broccoli, look at my beautiful hair, oh here's a big mouth... don't eat me no, no no!!!" As you take a bite. Let your tot do round two.
- Let them get hungry! – It's okay for kids to get a bit hungry. Set mealtimes and stick to them. Then, serve the veggies first. Your first bite of food is always the tastiest; capitalize on that and make it a healthy vegetable.
- Master chefs - Allow your child to be your sous chef in making the meal. Spark their curiosity in trying their concoction. As much exposure to the food as possible will make them more likely to try it.
- Sneak them in - Blended soups and shakes are great for hiding the healthy greens that some kids like to avoid.
- Be opportunistic - Pools and playgrounds are great at making kids ravenous and more likely to try anything

you put in front of them. Take a veggie tray to the pool instead of chips.

3. BATHROOM

This third step is straightforward. Do you need to use the bathroom? Have you been delaying all morning simply because you had too much on your plate?

As an adult, I expect you can identify and fix that problem very quickly, so I won't talk too much about this. There are plenty of physical and emotional repercussions of holding off for too long, and you probably know them all.

Now this may not apply to all kids and not all stages of toddlerhood. When my twins first learned to use the potty, they had accidents without blinking their eyes. There were no signs at all that they might need to use the bathroom.

As they got older, the signs were a lot more noticeable. If I did happen to miss them or the kids were too distracted to notice their own body signs, they inevitably became very whiny. It got to the point where whenever my oldest daughter Izzy had big crying episodes, her bladder would soon release.

My youngest daughter Lily however, would run up to me and just whine "Mommy, Mommy, Mommy" over and over. I wouldn't know what she wanted. An accident would follow not long after.

I started noticing a pattern. She sensed something going on in her body and needed a little assistance to get to the toilet. So whenever she came to me whining, if she was well-rested and not hungry, we'd head to the bathroom if she hadn't gone in a while.

One particular morning, she was unbearably clingy. She was moaning, groaning, and wanting to be carried around. After a couple of hours, she finally went to the bathroom and pooped.

When she was done, she got off the potty, and without any prompt, she walked upstairs and happily played alone for a while.

Finally! You can imagine my relief.

4. HEALTH

Next up is health. No one operates at 100% when feeling sick. It's hard enough to constantly keep your cool with toddlers without throwing in a cold or flu or even your period.

If you're sick, then it's time to call in the reinforcements. Or better yet, send the kids to their grandparents or friends for a few hours.

If that's not possible, then try to minimize your workload. Order takeout, don't do any chores, and conserve all your energy for dealing with your children. Spend the day playing or reading with them. It'll be a lot easier to keep them happy and keep you relaxed.

Now, sick toddlers are pretty easy to identify when they're in the thick of it. But at the beginning of the sickness, you might have difficulty figuring out why your child is acting fussy. Common signs include sleeplessness, having trouble settling down, whining, losing appetite, feeling cold, looking unusually flushed or pale, and losing interest.

If you suspect your toddler might be getting sick, dress them warmly, make some yummy chicken soup or some herbal tea, and load them up with vitamin D. Best to nip it in the bud if possible.

If your tots aren't feeling well, you can expect them to be more needy and whiny. Unfortunately, there's no quick fix for that. Give them a lot of love and affection, it will make them feel emotionally better, if not physically, and less prone to meltdowns.

I remember when my toddlers got a cold that was quickly followed by strep throat. It was the most miserable two weeks that our family had to endure up until that point. Sick kids turn into sleepless kids, especially if they have stuffy noses, which in turn become sleepless parents, and now no one's physical needs are met.

Healthy food, help, and patience are the only cures.

Preventative health

Prevention is indeed the best medicine. By taking care of our bodies and our children's bodies, we can get ahead of any sicknesses and reduce the chances of catching any bugs. Plenty of exercise, vegetables and fruits, vitamins, and consistent self-care will do wonders for everyone.

Make sure that you and your children have plenty of outdoor time. Fresh air and sunshine are irreplaceable.

Take care of your body. It is the temple of your mind and soul. You will deteriorate if it does.

CREATING A ROUTINE FOR CONSISTENT CARE

Routines are a great way to ensure your toddlers' physical and emotional needs are met. In my experience, parents either love routines or hate them.

My love of routines started with the twins; believe it or not, it had nothing to do with kids. It allowed me to skip out on certain tedious family obligations because we had to stick to the twins' schedule. When my third was born, I started to love routines because I knew there was relief in sight since the kids all napped daily from 11:30 to 2 p.m. It was my special time of peace and quiet. But enough about me. What about the kiddos?

Routines and schedules have a considerable impact on toddlers' growth. It helps babies and toddlers develop self-control.

They find comfort and security in daily routines—activities that happen at about the same time and in the same way every day. This is especially true for toddlers with autism or any other developmental concern.

They benefit emotionally from knowing when it is time to play, eat, sleep, or expect a loved one to return. It instills in them the belief that caring adults will consistently meet their needs. By feeling secure and well-cared for, children can engage themselves in their "job" of playing, exploring, and learning. They are then free of worry or doubt, and, therefore, come find you, whine and nag a lot less.

Having a routine also helps decrease power struggles and increase bonding. She can anticipate upcoming events. As a result, she feels secure and in charge, like when you say, "It's time to come inside and have lunch," she already knows that lunch comes after playing outside and is not caught off guard. She won't fight you on it. She also knows when her next outdoor playtime will be, making her more likely to comply with a less favorable request, coming inside.

> Anna, mom of 1, and caretaker of 4: "The kids do so great at nap time - most days - because they know it's coming. Even if they are disappointed it's time for a nap, they don't usually fight me."

Routines can also cut down on the number of reprimands and "nos" since your child knows what should happen next:

"I understand you're excited to play with your toys. However, it's time to get ready for bed. Remember, after we brush our teeth and put on our pajamas, it's storytime."

> Lily from Vancouver, mom of 1: "Mia is now 15 months old; she drinks milk every night at 7:30. We play for a bit on the floor as she drinks,

her dad gives her a bath, we read a book, say a prayer, and she's in bed by 8:15. Lately, when she finishes her milk, she smiles big and waves to me as she walks upstairs, which shows me she knows that the nightly ritual is beginning."

Routines also create predictable patterns to which the child can apply logic and reason. For example, we wash our hands before eating to be clean. Washing hands = cleanliness.

As kids get older, they expand their social circles. They meet more people and assimilate patterns and routines for getting along with them.

Children who adhere to patterns at home also adapt far more readily to school schedules since they are less likely to feel overwhelmed and restless throughout the day since they see their home as a safe haven.

Routine encounters that develop social skills include saying "hello" and "goodbye" and chit-chatting with others. These exchanges also allow us to help our kids learn how to talk.

As for us parents, having a set routine may provide a sense of fulfillment. Sure, routines help children adjust to change, but they also make parenting easier for us adults. We know when to schedule appointments, when the kids will be hungry, when the tantrums are more likely to happen, etc.

Most of us view everyday routines as mundane tasks. But they are a great way to help your child learn and grow while they develop healthy habits.

We brush our teeth every night before bed. We bring our dishes to the sink after dinner. We get dressed and make our bed in the morning.

As I mentioned earlier, your sponge-brain child is absorbing all of this and normalizing it. These "chores" are becoming normal things we care about every day.

If you're getting some pushback in your routines, consider removing yourself from the equation. Go online and download our Toddler Picture Routine Checklist for morning and night, or order it online. It's laminated, a.k.a. toddler-proof. You can stick it on the wall and empower your child to take charge of his own routine by following the checklist and completing his tasks.

SAMPLE SCHEDULE FOR YOUR TODDLER

Need help putting together a schedule for your toddler? Take this plan and change it to fit your family's needs. If your kid spends time at a daycare, ask about their routines so you can coordinate with them.

7:00 a.m. Wake up, potty, and cuddle in bed

7:30 a.m. Breakfast time & cleanup

8:00 a.m. Get dressed, potty, make beds, and brush teeth

8:30 a.m. Parent-led activity (craft, dancing, etc) or special time

9:15 a.m. Potty, wash hands, followed by snack time

9:45 a.m. Independent play/mom makes lunch and preps dinner

10:45 a.m. Outdoor time

11:30 a.m. Lunch, followed by story time

12:00 p.m. Potty, naptime, or quiet rest

2:30 p.m. Potty, wash hands, followed by an afternoon snack

3:00 p.m. Outdoor play or take a nature walk

4:30 p.m. Potty, followed by a parent-led activity or special time

5:00 p.m. Make dinner, play, clean up or help with dinner. Eat.

6:15 p.m. Potty, bath time, and teeth and hair brushing

7:00 p.m. Pajamas, read a bedtime story, and sing a lullaby

7:30 p.m. Potty, settle into bed for a peaceful night's sleep

CHAPTER 3

Meeting Emotional Needs

Little Bodies, Big Emotions

I laugh when people call my two-year-old a baby. Babies don't get into your makeup and finger paint the wall; babies won't intentionally hit you; babies don't wait for you to turn your back to grab a chair, climb onto the counter, and start chugging a jar of maple syrup (true story). My little feisty two-year-old… a baby? I don't think so. She is a blossoming toddler.

She navigates life in a way that the rest of us secretly hope we could—with confidence, insistence, and absolute conviction that she is the center of the universe.

When my three babies turned into toddlers, a magical transformation took place. Gone were my ever-obedient munchkins, and hello to these constantly curious little creatures incapable of hearing the word "no."

They adore laughter and playfulness. But our humor did not always align…

A favorite activity of theirs was destroying my perfectly arranged bookshelves and lining up the books on the floor in a path-like pattern so they could pretend they were walking on a bridge.

An innocent and fun activity that I wouldn't have had a problem with if the books made it back to the shelf without having each page ripped out because they enjoyed watching me tape things back together.

But that is only one of many of their so-called fun activities.

Their curiosity always gets the best of them, or, in reality, us. Ever wonder what is going on in that curious little brain? It must sound something like this:

"What would happen if I pushed this mug off this counter?"

"Ohh these buttons feel funny! Let's push them all at the same time!"

"Oh here's mom's phone; I want to pretend to be Mommy!"

"Oh oops, the phone fell down..."

"I'm gonna put the car keys in my little purse up in my room; that's what Mommy does."

And so the treasure hunt begins!

Being the mom of a toddler is a wild adventure filled with love, joy, and some seriously mind-boggling challenges.

As if sleepless nights, constant messes, and temper tantrums weren't enough, a recent Mayo Clinic study revealed that mothers of young children face a risk of mental health problems. Around 19% of mothers report experiencing two or more depressive symptoms.

Depression is a serious issue and can become a chronic problem. It's like that unwanted guest who overstays their welcome at your chaotic family gathering.

Not only does maternal mental health impact moms themselves, but it also wields a powerful influence on the health and development of our little ones. It's like a magical bond that connects the two of you in an unbreakable chain of emotions.

It's called the mirroring effect.

Children watch their parents and take on their behaviors as their own. So, ensuring mom's well-being becomes crucial to raising a healthy, happy child.

WHAT HAPPENS WHEN YOU NEGLECT SELF-CARE?

I was complaining to my mother one day about all the struggles and challenges I was facing with having four children ages three and under at home. It seemed like I was spending all day cooking and cleaning. Come five o'clock my husband would come home and the house was a dirty mess.

All of my hard work, and there was nothing to show for it!

Then the "bad" feelings would start. "I'm such a failure. My house never stays tidy. The kids don't listen to me. Maybe I wasn't cut out for motherhood."

My mom echoed my frustrations and said, "Every task that a mother does is quickly undone." It rang true.

You take an hour to cook a meal, only for it to be consumed in ten minutes. Thirty minutes of cleaning can be undone by a five-second-tornado child.

It can feel incredibly unfulfilling to watch and live through the quick destruction of your accomplishments, day after day, as your toddlers grow.

If you were going to work, you would experience a sense of accomplishment and satisfaction at the end of each day. You would feel successful. The positive feelings would come in daily.

But at home, this is not the case. Motherhood is tough work. The result is usually hard to see since it can take weeks or months for your toddler to master a new skill or get out of a funky phase.

You become stuck in the daily rabbit hole routine of cleaning, cooking, and managing the children, only to start over the very next day. Many parents do wind up feeling trapped in an ongoing loop of caring for their children while having little time for themselves.

I know I did.

After spending a few weeks on my husband's crazy sixty-hour week schedule, I was ready to lose it. I had turned into a full-blown knee-jerk reactive parent. Yelling, screaming, threatening, I did it all, and none of it was working.

My kids were testing the limits - it was a game of one-upmanship! They had me on my toes, trying to stay calm and composed as they challenged every boundary. I couldn't help but admire their determination... even if it drove me up the wall.

My oldest son, Anthony, decided he was a budding Picasso - his meals were painted across the walls, cheeks, and floors! His messy artistry had us seeing food in all new ways.

Chaos ensued when his twin, Izzy, didn't get what she wanted. Potty's full of pee were dumped on the floor, doors were slammed, my couches were bit. Nothing was off limits to her uncontrollable fits of rage.

Lily kicked it up a notch too. She was getting into all of my toiletries, and painting herself and the furniture with it. Did you know that toothpaste removes paint from wood? I didn't know that. Imagine my surprise when all the paint started coming off the dresser when I finally got around to wiping the toothpaste off it.

It was a vicious cycle. The more they acted out, the angrier I got, which would, in turn, fuel their wild escapades.

I had to break this spiral of bad behavior, and it all started with me.

I needed a chance to relax away from my kids so that the next time they acted up, Mama could be ready! A much-needed timeout - for both them AND me - seemed like just what we needed.

The comedian Jim Gaffigan was asked what it was like to have 5 kids. His reply, "Imagine you're drowning. And someone hands you a baby."

That was me. I was drowning. And seeing my kids all so desperate for my attention, I would never allow myself a minute on my own.

Do you believe you're a better mother when you put your kids first?

I know I did. I would feel guilty for needing a break from them, for wanting to go to the grocery store, the gym or a walk by myself. How could I when all these kids needed me, and I barely had enough time for them?

I was so wrong.

The pace I was setting for myself as a mother was not sustainable. If motherhood was being stranded in the desert, then "mom time" was sips of water that would allow me to endure the desert.

No matter what, you should always put yourself first. I understand that it is easier said than done. I struggled to see that. My mother gave us kids her all, from sunrise till sundown. She was always there for us. That's what I grew up with. And I wanted to always be there for my children, too.

The problem was that it clearly wasn't working since I was unhappy, my energy level was dipping, and my patience was thinning.

It took a big fight with my husband and him yelling at me to take some time for myself for me to take a step back and realize how important it is not just for me, but also for my marriage and my children.

When self-care is neglected, everything else that stems from it suffers, too. All of this begins within and then radiates outside. If we adults only see the empty side of the glass, how can we expect our kids to see the full side? How can we, as parents, instill optimism in our children if we don't feel it?

If we can't find joy in life, how can we expect our children to?

How well you care for yourself greatly impacts how well you care for your children and other family members.

To keep the home environment pleasant, we need to develop emotional maturity, ensuring that our moods and actions do not spoil the atmosphere at home. A balanced and fulfilling life shapes our overall well-being. To bring that balance, we cannot allow our lives' social, mental, spiritual, and physical aspects to suffer.

Upon realizing this, any mother would also agree that in addition to her many other duties, which include parenting, she also has certain obligations to herself. We refer to this as "self-responsibility."

Taking care of yourself on a daily basis won't hurt your career or family life. Do a quick search online, and you'll discover that successful entrepreneurs all have a daily healthy self-care routine.

Self-care encompasses maintaining a well-rounded schedule for yourself, which fosters a well-rounded state of mind.

We, as individuals, have a fundamental obligation to put our needs first, and there shouldn't be any shame, self-pity, or guilt attached to doing so. Only when we prioritize self-nurturing can we effectively care for others.

After all, being a parent can be draining at times. You need to refuel to be armed for the next round.

Let's be real here; I'm not talking about taking 3 hours a day to yourself (Or if you have one child and can afford to do that while they nap or are with a sitter, great!). I am advocating for at least 10 to 15 minutes, or more if you can, where you are consciously doing something to help you physically, mentally, or spiritually. For example, a stretching routine, small workout, journaling, reading a book, prayer time, etc…

I'll be frank: scrolling through your news feed or various social media platforms does not count. Those things are entertainment, not contributors that would improve your mind, body, and soul. And honestly, they often result in negative feelings regarding your life or looks.

THE MIRRORING EFFECT

A continuous "mirroring effect" is at work in relationships between parents and children. Whether it happens instantly or gradually, conscious or unconscious, our children exhibit behaviors acquired through a psychological process called "observational learning."

When they are young, they are open to what they see, and repeat it. And they unconsciously see their parents as examples to follow. It's how they learn how to behave, interact with people, and what's expected in society. It's even how they learn to talk. They are essentially mimicking your words and tone of voice, and are learning to match them correctly with their emotions. So what to say and how to sound when they feel a certain way. These assimilations are learned through observational learning. That is why it is imperative to model the behavior you want to see in your children and to model self-care so our children can learn the importance of caring for one's mind, body, and soul at a young age.

Hannah from Georgia - Mom of 1: "I think a lot about how my mom was so completely negative about her looks, and I grew up thinking it was weird to consider yourself pretty. I now realize how messed up that is, and I'm always wanting to make sure my daughter doesn't hear me speak negatively about my looks. When she says 'my dress is so pretty,' I'm like 'yeah, we look great.'"

PRIORITIZING SELF-CARE AS PARENTS

There are three main reasons why parents should prioritize self-care:

1. Fosters Healthy Family Bonds

    It helps parents, particularly moms, maintain healthy family bonds, which contributes to lowering the likelihood of kids having mental health problems.

2. Helps Child Build a Self-Identity & Maintain Parent Self-Identity

    Creating some distance between parent and child is crucial for developing the child's sense of self in those early years. But as our kids get older and reach puberty, they develop into unique individuals, and it is then our turn to separate from them.

    Taking time for ourselves throughout the years allows us to examine how closely our sense of self is entangled with our children's. When we take a step back and look at our lives, we see that being a parent shapes much of what we do and think about ourselves. We need to make sure that we know who we are and don't feel lost when we become empty-nesters (a.k.a. the kids are out of the house).

3. Setting The Example

    We must set a good example for our children by living healthy lifestyles. Children learn to care for themselves by watching their parents care for themselves. Our kids need to know how to deal with stress and difficulties in life by doing things that help them feel better about themselves.

Practicing self-care without feeling guilty

Taking care of yourself is not selfish; it is necessary. So, if you're the kind of person who tends to put others first and neglect your own needs in the process - it's time for a change! Remind yourself that taking care of your well-being comes before anything else. It's a marathon, not a sprint. You don't want to run yourself ragged until you're burnt out and have nothing left to give. Prioritizing yourself will mean more energy and a greater capacity to give back later down the line. Don't let yourself run until there's nothing left — invest wisely!

The best example of this would be the airplane oxygen mask. If you've ever been on a plane, you know that in an emergency, masks will appear. They emphasize that all adults put their masks on first before assisting children.

Is that an unnecessary precaution, or is it purely logical that you can only help others once you've secured your safety?

If you try helping the toddler first, you might find yourself out of air before you can complete the job, and then you're both in peril.

I know what you're thinking now: "Don't be dramatic. That's a life and death scenario; we're talking about everyday life here."

The stakes are just as high for everyday life. Raising a well-rounded, capable human being takes constant effort and dedication. As the parent, you set the example your kids will follow, so make sure they learn how to meet their physical and mental needs - not just for today but also in preparation for whatever life throws at them down the line.

Your actions speak louder than words – showing is a more powerful learning tool than telling! Demonstrate how to obtain balance and stay healthy, then watch as your child follows suit.

Joining parent-peer groups.

Sometimes, being a parent becomes hard work and causes us to question our abilities, especially when things go wrong. When this happens, we can get help from parent-peer groups where we'll find people going through similar experiences. Finding a support network helps alleviate the sense of being isolated, making it easier to tackle the challenges of being a parent.

If you don't have a local parent group or can't get to one, try checking out some online parent groups. There's a plethora of them on Facebook.

Creating a "me-time" routine.

Giving yourself a few minutes of "me-time" every day is essential. You may use this time to do things you like or sometimes to do nothing at all. It's a chance to be by yourself and think things over - your mind, body and soul time. "Me-time" helps us reset our brains, relax, focus better, and be more effective. It also helps us figure out how to solve problems and improves our relationships. If you're like me and can't seem to get a moment to yourself, consider waking up fifteen minutes before the rest of the crew so you can start your day with your "me-time".

Need some ideas for your "me-time"? Ask yourself these questions: What does my body need? Stretching, exercising, a daily walk, perhaps? What does my mind need? A crossword puzzle with some coffee in the a.m., reading a book, playing an instrument? What does my soul need? Prayer, meditation, time in nature, journaling, a daily good deed.

Personal retreat.

We all need a mental and spiritual reset from time to time, and a personal retreat - such as meditation, yoga, spa therapy, or taking singing or dancing classes - can do just that.

Dating with the spouse.

Without question, the connection with our spouse is one of the most crucial relationships we need to maintain. The demands of parenting can damper a couple's ability to enjoy the romantic side of their love for one another. Which is, after all, the reason the family exists.

I'm a big believer that spousal dating should happen every week. And that there should be a no-kid-talk rule during said dates. Take time together, keep the flame alive, and be in love. It's the best gift you can give your children. Showing them what a healthy, happy marriage looks like.

Don't dwell too much on this if you're a single parent. Simply show your child how you love yourself and take care of yourself.

When to seek help.

In a culture that emphasizes self-sufficiency and takes pleasure in independence, it can be hard to ask for help. But reaching out may sometimes be life-saving, and the inability to do so can leave us anxious, facing avoidable repercussions.

Some people think that parents should just know how to be good parents and not need help from anyone else. But how can you possibly master a skill without learning it and practicing it?

You can set the bar high but don't have to get there alone and take the long way. Not when you're raising another human being and the stakes are high. Remember, nobody is perfect. Asking for help doesn't mean that you are lacking. It just means you have the courage, self-awareness, and humility to know you need more.

When parenting becomes challenging, one valuable skill is "delegation." Delegating a small amount of responsibility to others like babysitters, grandparents, or a daycare goes a long way in alleviating the stress involved with modern-day parenting.

However, if the tension becomes too much and your mental health is at stake, just pick up the phone. In this modern era, professional help is only one phone call away. You can find a plethora of therapists online or in person. Virtual therapy, also known as telehealth, is growing fast. You can have virtual appointments right from your home. Talking to a professional can help solve problems that seem impossible to solve. Embrace the reality that being a parent can be both thrilling and draining, and understand that it is okay to ask for assistance when needed.

I know I've spent a good chunk of time in this chapter, but before we move forward, I want you to understand that everything starts here. All of the help and strategies in this book - or any other parenting book for that matter - will be hard, if not impossible, to implement if you as a parent are not prioritizing yourself.

> Sara from California - mom of 4 : "I have to do my daily stretches, it energizes me and helps me regroup. The kids try to climb on me as I do them but I manage to distract them and take care of myself. If I didn't do that every day, I wouldn't survive my chaotic house."

I can attest to this. I was a "knee-jerk reaction" parent - as my husband likes to call it- until I made the changes to prioritize self-care. I could only react to my children rather than proactively deal with their various needs. I was unhappy; my kids were therefore mirroring my behavior and were also unhappy. And I spent my days putting out fires and surviving rather than building a garden and thriving.

At my husband's insistence, I finally said the chores had to wait, and while the kids napped, I started a daily fifteen-minute workout routine - to help my body heal from four back-to-back births. My husband and I started our weekly date night. We set aside a little money to get help to keep up with the chores and laundry. I immersed myself in podcasts and books to learn about the various toddler issues in my house.

Things got better.

The interesting thing was, they got better overnight, simply because once I started taking care of myself and was happier, so were the kids. And everything got easier from there on out.

Why did it take me so long to prioritize self-care?

I'm sure some philosopher or therapist would have a better answer, but perhaps we feel undeserving of self-love, or we feel the pressure to be perfect and can't stop to pause and wonder what it really is that we need to reach the best version of ourselves... Food for thought. Let's move on.

MEETING A TODDLER'S BASIC EMOTIONAL NEEDS

So, what does your kid emotionally need to flourish at this pivotal age?

I'll clue you in. Attention, attention, and more attention.

Not just any attention - the right kind of attention from their primary caretaker, which in most cases is the mother.

They crave attention so much that they will get it by any means necessary. If you don't give it to them at the right time and in the right way, then they will demand it from you when they act out. And if that cycle is not corrected, the negative behaviors will keep escalating until it becomes the only way they try to get attention, or the child simply gives up on the relationship.

Now, I'm not saying that all negative behavior is for attention, but a HUGE part is.

Which brings us to the foundation of the mother-child relationship:

Quality bonding time.

If you think about it, it's the foundation of any relationship; whether it be between friends, spouses, or a mother-child bond. It's how we stay connected to each other - because if love could talk, quality time would be its language!

For kids, this precious interaction with their mothers can help them feel secure in themselves while fostering confidence and registering the essential message that they are valued above all else.

BONDING TIME

What does bonding time look like? Well, let's think back on our adult relationships.

I feel the happiest and most secure in my marriage when my husband and I spend some quality time together. It doesn't feel as fulfilling if our time together gets interrupted. If we spend the entire time arguing or discussing a particular problem, then the time spent together doesn't fuel our bond. Likewise, if we have a third wheel, even if it's one of our little monkeys, it doesn't feel like quality time at all. And most importantly, If we go too long without spending quality time together, our relationship suffers.

It's no different with your child. The same parameters that apply to your relationship with adults also cover your relationships with your children. And here they are:

- One on one. This means one adult, one child - no third wheel allowed!
- Uninterrupted time together
- High in frequency, daily is ideal
- Doing a fun/bonding activity that's free of technology
- Defined to your child, "This is our special time for the next 10/15 minutes."
- The child picks the activity
- No technology

Now, I'm not asking you to set aside an hour every day for each child; I know I would never be able to do that; a simple 10 minutes will do. If you can do more than that, great! Just remember that if you have multiple children to keep the time equal amongst them all. It is also important to inform your child that this is your special time with them, and you are so excited to spend it with them.

When we first started spending consistent bonding time with our children, we saw a drastic behavior change. Izzy, who had a habit of following me all over the house and never leaving my side, started spending a few hours happily playing independently. The kids were getting along better because they were secure in the fact that they would all be getting attention from us, and so they stopped competing for it.

I distinctly remember a very chaotic morning when Izzy was crying and wailing for no apparent reason. My husband crouched beside her and asked, "Do you need to do special time?" Between her sobs, she managed to choke out a "yeah." He picked her up and took her upstairs to read some books, and that was the end of that.

You can offer your child suggestions for your special time activity, but let them pick what to do. As long as it's not a technology-related choice, then you can't go wrong.

Bonding time is the cornerstone of your parenting. It is the perfect preventative tool for most behavioral issues you might be facing. Again, prevention is the best medicine. It's no different for emotional medicine.

You can also use this amazing tool as an emergency behavior fix. When my youngest son Jamie was born, things were a bit chaotic. He wasn't nursing correctly and kept losing weight, so I was naturally preoccupied with getting him back on track.

My daughter Lily was having a hard time with all the changes. Out of nowhere, she developed a stutter. She was so upset with her inability to communicate easily that after a few days, she stopped talking altogether. I was heartbroken. I knew it was normal for children to go through regressions when a new baby comes into the fold, but it wasn't any easier to watch.

I was desperate to help her. I tried everything I could find online, from encouraging speech to repeating the sentences back to her to singing together. There was no quick fix.

Then, one day, I decided to try something new. I did three special time sessions with her in one day. I made sure to emphasize my excitement at doing so much special time. The next morning, she talked to her sister. It was just one sentence, but it was enough to give me hope. So I kept going. After a week of three special time sessions a day, she was back to her usual, very chatty self. I was speechless - no pun intended.

This one-on-one time is the most powerful tool for toddler behavior. Do not underestimate it.

HOW TO ACHIEVE EMOTIONAL WELLBEING IN TODDLERS

It may be self-evident, but it bears repeating: to survive, children need love. Your love and comfort provide a safe haven from which your child learns and grows.

This is not just feel-good advice; a child's physical, mental, and emotional developments are all positively affected by the love, attention, and compassion they get in their first few years of life.

There is a mountain of research to back this up. Dr Harley Rotbart, from the Pediatrics at Childrens in Colorado believes that contact and affection encourage brain growth in infants and young children.

What is the most effective method of expressing affection? Give your youngster plenty of hugs, pats on the back, smiles, words of encouragement, attention, and playtime.

When your toddler is unhappy, act quickly to help them get to a happier place. By doing this, you are not "caving in" but encouraging your child to learn good emotional management. Young children form a healthy bond when they feel cared for, which helps their brains grow.

There are things that can harm your child's emotional well-being. The main one is media, . Much can be said about media and its negative effects on children's developing brains. Not only does it negatively affect their social skills and ability to focus, but it also causes health problems, speech delays, and deficiencies. Furthermore, staring at a screen causes overstimulation and stunts your child's creativity.

It can be so tempting to turn the TV on or hand the child the phone or iPad when you need them to be cooperative or quiet, but the truth is, you can achieve the same with a new book or a sketch pad without causing your child a disservice.

In the next chapter, we'll discuss communicating with your toddler as the second best (after bonding time) preventative tool for power struggles, tantrums, and sibling rivalry.

CHAPTER 4

Communication

Decipher Toddler Code

From the moment we find out we're expecting, we know that we will work our hardest to give our kid the best life we can give them. We think of the best toys and schools for their cognitive development and sports and playgrounds for physical development. Yet, we often overlook their emotional development. We assume that they're somehow supposed to learn that as they grow or that it'll be easier to teach them about emotions when they are older.

I remember thinking, "oh, they'll grow up and learn to share," or "When they're a bit older, then we can start teaching them how to be polite and considerate."

Our children's emotional and social growth is just as vital, if not more, than their physical and cognitive growth. Their chances of integrating well into society and thriving in a community rely heavily on their emotional and social development. Healthy communication skills are the pillars of success.

So why wait till later to teach these vital skills? We've already established that toddlers are like sponges and have a super brain that allows them to learn pretty much anything at this young age. So why would we wait until they are set in their ways? It gets harder to learn things as you grow older. Have you ever tried teaching your parents or grandparents how to use a smartphone?

My son Anthony was born with certain physical anomalies. We always knew that he would face some physiological challenges, but as he grew, we wondered about other challenges he might face. We suspected that he might be on the autism spectrum. One of the professionals we spoke with emphasized the importance of therapy at a young age. She said, "We want him to be in therapy before school age because we're trying to teach him good emotional and social behavior. It is so important and beneficial for these children when they are young. We see a lot of cases where teachers or parents just wait and expect the kid to "catch on". Those kids, that are swept under the rug, are the kids that grow up to struggle as adults."

COMMUNICATION GOAL FOR DISCIPLINE

The problem with blaming,
shaming, or using pain to discipline.

Children need to learn about social standards and appropriate behavior. They have to figure out how to get along with others. Our job is to teach them how and to discipline them accordingly.

So your kids always know what is expected of them and what their limitations are, discipline should be fair and consistent. It will give them the emotional confidence to develop social and emotional growth.

Discipline methods based on fear do not teach children self-control.

They make the child resentful and angry with the parent and completely take away the learning experience, which is what discipline is all about.

Not convinced?

Imagine this: At work, your boss reminds you to be timely. Each day before you leave, he says, "8 a.m. sharp. Don't be late, or I'll give your job to someone who appreciates it more." You might be offended by a few things:

1. The assumption that you'll be late
2. The assumption that you need to be reminded so much
3. The threat of loss of job- which can also be very destabilizing

You might also fantasize about being late just to annoy him and see what he does. It's human nature, just like how a "Don't Touch" sign makes you want to touch even more. Just a little tap. Ha! I touched it! I showed them!

Also, imagine that you were 10 minutes late one morning. Your boss calls you out in the meeting in front of your coworkers and says, "You are never on time. You're ungrateful and don't deserve this job. I'm giving your project to Steven to manage."

Did you learn your lesson? Are you never going to be late again?

Or are you fuming?

"I had a flat tire! It wasn't even my fault," or "He's such an a**" or "Maybe I should just quit; I'm clearly not a good fit here." Can you notice how none of these thoughts are about being on time?

We'll discuss later on what exactly should be said in those moments.

Children need time to learn that they are responsible for what they do and that what they do has an effect. They are free to make their own decisions and choices (within reason); they are not, however, free of the consequences of those choices. An even-handed, reassuring approach to discipline at home will help teach them about responsibility.

Love

A crucial aspect of love we often overlook is being present and listening to our loved ones—an exchange of meaningful interaction.

The saying, "Actions speak louder than words," is well known for its wisdom and truth. In the case of parenting, especially positive parenting, I find that words are just as important as actions.

Your kid won't care if you're working your butt off to put them in dance or piano, buy them the best toys, or send them to the best school, not if they don't have any quality time with you.

All your actions will be for nothing without the simple exchange of meaningful words.

"How are you doing?" or "You sound upset. Would you like to talk about it?"

We cannot allow our children's feelings to go unnoticed, not if we're trying to raise emotionally healthy human beings.

Uniqueness

In nurturing our children's development, it's essential to acknowledge and embrace their uniqueness. Kids need to be free to be themselves.

We parents unwillingly put our children into boxes. Especially when we're talking with our parents on the phone or when we're with some friends:

"Oh, she's the shy one,"

"Sam is very aggressive,"

"Janie doesn't like asparagus."

These statements are detrimental to your children. Not only are you putting them in a box inside your mind, but you're also putting a box in their minds.

"I'm shy; I shouldn't say hello. My sister is the outgoing one,"

"I guess I'm an aggressive boy; I like hitting and being rough,"

"I don't like asparagus - why bother trying it?"

To embracethe uniqueness of our children we must give them the freedom to explore their own limits, without imposing preconceived labels. This approach ensures that our parenting is free from prejudice, allowing them to develop without artificial barriers constraining their capabilities.

Acceptance, Recognition, and Approval

When we give our kids unconditional love, they learn that they're accepted just as they are. The confidence boost they get from this is invaluable as they continue their educational path. "Mom and Dad love me, regardless of how many friends I have how smart I am, or how hard I work."

If you want your child to develop a sense of self-worth, your acceptance and approval of them should never be conditional. It should be automated and unrelated to their strengths and achievements.

HOW TO DISCIPLINE POSITIVELY

Can you feel the weight of the rock bearing down on your shoulders?

I certainly do. Every day, I wonder if I'm doing enough, if I've let one of my kids down, or if I've failed in some aspect. It can feel crushing. That's why I started this journey into positive discipline - to alleviate the burden.

I want to dedicate the rest of this chapter to this singular, most powerful tool in gentle parenting. Talking. That's the basis of positive parenting. Using dialogue to discipline children, to teach children right from wrong.

You might think, "I don't need someone to tell me how to talk to my kid." I would argue that in this modern era of screens and technology, we could all use some help improving our communication skills. More so for communication with emotionally unstable little people. After all, there are graduate degrees dedicated to communication, so I'm sure we all could improve some.

A cousin came to me not long ago, stating she wanted to stop spanking her kids. She'd gotten this "great" tip from a relative. She said, "Auntie A told me I shouldn't spank their butts because that's a private part. Instead, she said to have them hold out their hand and hit their palm with a wooden spoon. If they talk back, then add more hits. Isn't that great?"

I flinched when I heard that. Ouch. That sounds painful. And yes, pain is a powerful deterrent. So, what's wrong with spanking or other physical chastisement?

Well, for starters, if you have a strong-willed child, it won't work. We went down that route as new parents. It didn't take us long to see that it didn't faze our kids or change their behavior. Not only that, but we would feel tremendous guilt and shame.

Guilt is not an emotion you should ever feel when parenting.

And from what I've seen, in most cases, when the parent has reached the point of spanking, they've lost their cool, they've had it, or they don't know what else to do. The parent has become a "knee-jerk reaction" parent, which can sometimes feel almost like abuse. It can also teach our children that it's okay to resort to violence when you're losing your grip on your emotions and can't find the words or tools to communicate with the other person.

We don't want to be reactive parents. We want to be proactive ones instead.

There's a whole other dilemma that arises, too. Do you escalate the severity of the spank with the disobedience? Spank harder when their disobedience is worse? What point is too much? And then what?

What happens when your child turns into a teenager? I'm definitely not going to spank a teenager. So how would I get them to listen?

To top it all off, how does that make our kids feel about us? We're supposed to be their safe haven, and yet we're teaching them that sometimes it's okay for the people that love them the most to hurt them physically?

You might be thinking that's a bit too far, or I'm rationalizing this too much. But I don't believe we can fully understand how deep into our psyche certain experiences are embedded and how they form us.

Childhood trauma can last well into adulthood. It's a startling fact revealed by the National Child Traumatic Stress Network, which explains that 78 percent of children experience more than one traumatic event before age five. These early experiences can shape the developing brain and lead to various challenges later on in life, such as emotional regulation, distorted perceptions, relationship difficulties, low self-esteem, and much more.

So what punishment can we use then? Time outs, withholding sweets, canceling favorite activities or outings? Should we use any of these?

No. We should not use any punishments.

Why not?

Simple, because we're trying to teach our children how to behave, not inflict a penalty on them for not passing the lesson or offending us.

Does that mean our children should be allowed to do whatever they want and whenever they want?

Heck no.

Then how do we get them to listen to me, behave, and not hit their sister or steal their brother's toy?"

We desperately need these very important things to run a happy household.

I hope that from this book, you'll gain effective communication so that your child can learn to develop positive inner motivators rather than negative ones.

I love seeing my kids share because they want to, not because I demanded they do "or else." I want my kids to grow up and not steal because they don't want to be thieves, not because they are scared of the police catching them. Do you see the difference?

EFFECTIVE COMMUNICATION (THE GOLD MINE)

Mastering the skill of talking to your child so they will listen is a crucial aspect of any discipline strategy. Your child learns how to talk to other people by watching how you speak to him. The following are some conversational pointers I've picked up through the years with my kids:

Get down to their level

Get down to your child's eye level and make direct eye contact before you tell him what to do. Help him learn to concentrate: "Hey, Emma, can I have your attention?" or "Alex, I need you to listen." Maintain the same posture and body language while your child is speaking. Be careful not to make your eye contact so strong that your kid interprets it as a form of control rather than a way to connect with him.

Address your kid

Begin your request by mentioning the child's name: "Lily, could you..." Make sure you have their attention if you're going to talk to them.

Keep it short

Include the important instruction in the first sentence. Your toddler may grow parent-deaf the more you babble on. One typical error in dialogue is to speak too much rather than listen. It sends the message to the kid that you don't really know what you want to say. She can divert your attention if she can keep you talking.

Avoid Baby talk

It can be easy to fall into the baby talk trap, especially if your toddler isn't very chatty. However, it is important to model typical dialogue in front of your child and speak with them normally. As they watch you talk with others, you'll unwittingly show them how conversations flow and expand their vocabulary. When you then talk to them with the same tone, you're setting the expectation that they are also to converse in that manner, and you're building their confidence that they can chat with you like any older person.

You don't need to talk loud and super slow; that's for the opposite population. Use basic short sentences, and throw in new words occasionally.

Common pitfall: referring to yourself as "Mommy." "Mommy is feeling tired." Your child knows who you are. Use I, me, and my, and show them that you understand they are capable, and get them used to proper sentence structure.

We want children to talk and learn how to express themselves.

Repeat back

Ask your child to repeat back your instruction. If he can't, it's because it's too long or hard. I use this particular trick when I'm introducing a new rule.

I had to take all four children to the grocery store with me; I was very, very nervous. Previous attempts hadn't gone well at all. When we got to the store, I turned the car off, looked at my children, and said. "We have a new rule. When you're in the grocery store with me, you have to stay in the shopping cart and can't touch anything. If this rule is broken, then we have to leave the store. Can you guys repeat that to me so I know we all understand the new rule." They all did. "We have to stay in the cart and not touch anything, or we will have to come back to the car." That grocery run was the easiest I had ever been on thus far, including the ones with sitters and my husband.

If your child can't quite repeat complex phrases, try a simpler one: "If I run away, then I don't get to come," or something similar.

Don't assume it's a one-and-done. Your child might need to repeat back the same rule a few times before he normalizes the behavior. For the next two months, every time we had to go to the store with kids, they had to remind me what the store rule was before we could leave the car.

Positive sentences instead of negative sentences

Instead of saying "no running," which only makes you want to run, you can try: "We walk inside the house." Notice how there's no mention of "run" the action you don't want them to do, and no use of the word "no."

When you overuse "no," two things happen. The first, it makes any sane person on the receiving end want to rebel; second, it desensitizes the child from the word "no," which you must use when an imminent threat is involved.

Calm Voice and Tone

Children thrive in a secure and peaceful environment. Screaming, yelling, and shouting all create a natural fight-or-flight response in our bodies. Especially when you're on the receiving end of the shouting; furthermore, if you're engaged in a power struggle with your child, losing your temper will give them a power trip. "Hah! I won! I got Dad to lose it." Use a calm voice to deliver requests or inform of consequences.

Like with the word no, kids can get desensitized from yelling, too. Save the yelling for real threats.

You also need to watch your tone. You wouldn't enjoy being ordered around, and your child won't either. Try keeping your tone light, just like you would with a friend when delivering commands or corrections.

First, the legs, then the mouth

Instead of yelling, "Put your legos away; it's time for a bath," walk over to where your child is playing and calmly but firmly inform them that it's almost time for their bath. Then, sit down next to them and appreciate their handiwork for a few minutes, showing genuine interest. Going to your child shows that you're serious about your request. If you don't go to your child, your child might think you're just expressing an opinion.

Be kind and respectful

Parents often fall into the mistake of treating their child like a dumb adult or just an annoying person.

"You're such a brat," "You're so whiny," "You are just so annoying."

Think about how much your kid can grasp. They might not know the exact definition of brat, but they can certainly understand what you mean by your tone of voice. You are their teacher; insulting them will only hurt their feelings and damage the teacher-pupil relationship, making your child less receptive to your teachings.

Another common mistake is asking a toddler, "Why did you do that?" Even most adults are unable to provide a satisfactory response to that question. Try, "Let's talk about what you did," instead, and help them talk through their emotions and actions.

Additionally, if your child is in the room, don't talk about them like they aren't there. "Oh, Megan doesn't like going to the zoo, she prefers the playground." Well, Megan is right there, so let's say "Megan, do you prefer the zoo or the playground?"or, "Megan was mentioning that she prefers the playground, is that right honey?"

Follow rhyme rules

"You can have fun when you're all done," or
"When the lamp is red, you must stay in bed."
Ask your kid to repeat the rhymes back to you.
Carefully pick words and sentences that open up their little brains and shut down their mouths.

The secret weapon - play

What is a toddler's favorite thing to do? Well... play, of course! Do you know what my favorite thing to do is? Weaponise theirs. I'll explain.

Animate objects

Izzy refuses to get dressed after bath time. I've asked her ten times already, yet she's still prancing around in her birthday suit with no interest in putting her pajamas on. Suddenly, I sit up straight and say, "Did you hear that?" She stops and looks curiously at me. I keep going, "I think it's coming from your room." She follows me to her bedroom. Me in a silly voice, "Pick me! Pick me!" then again in my normal voice, "It's coming from your drawer!" I pull out two sets of pajamas and hold them up. I use my best silly voice and make the pajamas fight over who gets to be worn. My three-year-old is now bubbling with excitement and quickly picks a pair and hurriedly gets them on.

Kids are full of imagination; bring a little of it to life by animating some objects, and you'll quickly find a happy, cooperative child.

The Lego bucket: "I'm hungryyyyy!!! Feed me some lego!"

Shampoo bottle: "Oh, I have some special magic soap today. It'll make your hair shine! Tip your head back!"

Use Stories

When the twins turned 3, they decided it was time for a vegetable rebellion. And Lily, wanting to be just like her big siblings, put a strike on the vegetables too.

One night, I looked out the window at dinner time and said, "Have you ever heard the story of the carrot that wanted friends?"

My kids love stories; they could happily listen to me tell them stories all day. They all instantly quieted and looked at me.

Izzy said, "Tell it to us." With my best innocent look, I said, "Oh, of course! Everyone, take a bite of your carrots, and we'll get started." And just like that, with a story to focus on, the kids ate their food while listening to a very poorly crafted story about the carrot that ran through the garden and made friends with all the over vegetables only to be picked and eaten by three hungry children.

Practice good listening

The best way to teach your child to listen well is to show them what good listening is. Start with things you know your child is interested in. Ask questions that don't just need a yes or no answer. Focus on the details. Encourage their curiosity about the world. Instead of asking, "Did you see a bird outside?" try asking, "What colors did you notice on the birds you saw today?" Listen to their answers and let them steer the conversation. You don't need to talk a lot; lend them an attentive ear and repeat back what they say to encourage them to speak more.

Tot, "Mom, I saw a squirrel!"

Mom, "You saw a squirrel?!" (with matched excitement)

Tot, "Yes! It was so fast…"

Problem-solving

Izzy went on strike. She did not want to wash her hair. And boy, did it need a wash. I sat down with her with a pen and paper and said, "Izzy, we have a problem, and I need your help finding a solution. Your hair needs to get washed, and you don't like taking showers. What can we do to solve that problem?" We sat down with a pen and paper, and I made a very basic drawing of a shower with a girl (the problem). I had to go first, since she didn't fully comprehend what we were doing, and started drawing out some solutions. Then I asked her for a few. We went through each solution until we found one that worked for both of us. In this case, the solution was: tipping her head back and using a cup so no water gets in her eyes. I had offered to do that a few times prior to this exercise to no avail. But since she was now a part of finding the solution, she was eager to try it.

Rules:

- Wait for your child to calm down before problem solving.
- All solutions need to be written down, even the silly ones.

- The chosen solution needs to be agreed upon by parent and child.

Pick your fights

Having too many rules is not good for your child or you. You need to show your child that you're serious about your rules. For that to happen, you need to be able to follow through with your directives. Don't threaten to take away their toy if you don't feel like following through with the threat. So pick and choose your battles wisely.

Too Many Questions

Does your child like to ask you Twenty thousand questions? Are most of them questions he could figure out on his own? It can be easy to get irritated when you're being interrogated about what seems like trivial matters. Instead of getting annoyed and trying to get rid of your child, flip the script around with, "What do you think?"

Child: "Mom, Mom, is this cup full? Is this water?"

Mom: "Hmm, what do you think?"

Prompt your child to think about his questions. If he already knows the answer, he shouldn't need your affirmation, which will help him build self-confidence. If he doesn't know the answer, this exercise might get his brain thinking or creative juices flowing.

Remember your please and thank yous

Even a toddler is capable of picking up the word "please." Insist that your kid uses manners. No child should ever think that good manners are unnecessary. Use the language with your kids that you would want them to use with you.

Teach your children emotions and empathy

Instead of "What did you do to your sister?!" try: "Your sister is crying, she is upset. What can we do to make her feel better?"

"Look at how happy your baby brother is! He is smiling and giggling."

Instead of "Why do you keep taking other kids' toys?! Just wait your turn!" say: "Jake looks angry; I don't think he is done playing with that truck. What should we do to fix that?"

The formula = recognize the emotion in others + let the solution come from your child.

This does two things - The first, not give any attention to the aggressor, so they don't learn to get attention from bad behavior. The second, teach children to make amends and fix their mistakes.

I feel statements

Another powerful way to teach children to express their emotions verbally is through I feel statements. Instead of, "Stop making messes! You're so annoying!" try, "I feel very annoyed and angry when I see messes." Instead of, "You keep taking my stuff without asking me," say, "I'm feeling angry that my stuff is used without my permission." You're then allowing your child to understand the emotional consequences of his actions. You are also modeling how to recognize the emotions in himself and express them without hitting or fighting.

Descriptive Praise and instruction

Descriptive Praise

Descriptive praise communicates two essential things to your child. The first is that you recognize their actions and hard work, and the second is that they are capable human beings and should take pride in themselves.

Show that you really see them and not just the label placed on them.

For example, instead of, "Oh, you're so beautiful," something the child has no control over, try, "You picked out your purple skirt and purple shirt to match it; how tasteful!" or "I see a little girl who brushed her teeth and her hair and got dressed. You're looking clean and fresh."

A couple of things to note about descriptive praise: first off, you're introducing new words to your child's vocabulary, always a bonus, and more importantly, you actually took the time to recognize the effort your child took rather than just dishing out a quick compliment.

"Nice drawing, honey" doesn't recognize the effort your child put into his art. Try, "I see a pink squiggly line, oh, and a green straight line that touches it, and look, there's some blue and purple on this side." Your child will truly feel seen, appreciated, and cared for.

For example, instead of "You're such a good boy," try: "Wow, you picked up all your dirty clothes and put them in the dirty laundry basket. You must be so proud of yourself." Instead of saying, "Mommy is so pleased with you" - which doesn't even mention the child or their actions - say, "Wow, you ate all your vegetables! Even those peas, and they're not even your favorite! You must be very proud of yourself."

You can also use praise to recognize the effort made and ask for more. "You didn't pick up all your toys. There's still some toys on the floor" can be substituted with, "I see the legos are back in their bin, and the blocks are in their box. Hooray! Oh, I see stuffed animals all over the floor."

An excellent tip to remember descriptive praise is by starting sentences with "I see…"

Descriptive commands

Descriptive commands are a great way to get your child to do your bidding without entering a power struggle or accidentally sounding whiny and exemplifying unwanted behavior. Instead of saying, "Mike, pick up your toys." You can say, "I see toys all over the floor." If you let the child fill in the holes, the lesson will likely stick.

"Izzy, bring your dirty plate to the sink." can be subbed with, "I see dirty plates still at the table."

Instead of "What's wrong with you!? You're always making messes." try, "I see a very messy room with some clothes on the floor, a few train tracks, a hairbrush, and a dirty cup." This is an excellent way of not butting heads with your child while pointing out all the things you'd like to see remedied.

This tool works great with a bit of playfulness as well. For example, "I see a sink hungry for dirty dishes!" "I see dirty hands that are looking for soap! Soap, soap, we need soap!"

No more bribes or threats

Bribes and threats always surface in our desperation. And that's the problem; children can sense our desperation and weakness, and it gives them a power kick. "If you get in the car, I'll play your favorite song." "If you finish your food, you can have chocolate." Or a negative, perhaps, "If you don't stop whining, then I'm going to put you in your room." "If you keep hitting your brother, I'm going to give you a swat on the butt."

Instead of saying "if" and coming from a point of weakness. Try using these sentence structures:

When (a certain less desired action is completed) then (a more pleasant action follows).

"When you've tidied up your toys, then we can read a book."

"When you've finished your meal, then we can go to the park and have fun on the swings."

"When your pajamas are on, teeth brushed, and hair combed, then we get to read some books."

"When," makes it clear that the task will happen, is better than the word "if," which gives the impression that the child has a choice even if you do not intend to provide him with one. Or that you are bribing him, which puts him in a position of power.

"When" can be substituted with "once" or "first."

"First, we finish our breakfast, then we can play trains."

"Once we take care of the laundry, then we get to go to the playground."

This is where a good schedule and routine can help you ensure you have all the fun stuff scheduled after the chores or family contributions are done.

Directives should start with "I want"

When you can't avoid the directive. Say, "I want you to bring me the ball" instead of, "'Bring me the ball.'" Instead of saying, "Give the toy to Sarah," let's say, "I want you to give the toy to Sarah now." This works well for kids who want to do the right thing but don't like being told what to do. When you say, "I want," you give a reason to do what you say instead of just giving an order.

Self-Pride

Feeling pride in our children's accomplishments and behavior is very normal. After all, we want our kids to grow up and be great! And if we're proud of them, then they must be great.

The problem arises when we start using our pride and approval as a tool to achieve a specific behavior. If our children are using other people's approval to feel self-worth, can they truly be happy pursuing the things they want?

Also, what happens if they pick the wrong role model? When toddlers become teenagers, social acceptance becomes very important and might override mommy and daddy's approval. If they are used to getting their self-worth externally, they might succumb to peer pressure or allow themselves to be influenced by the wrong people. A scary thought, especially when you see how sexuality is pushed onto teenagers at a very young age.

Instead, let's teach our children to have self-pride and inner drive. When they do something worth praising, instead of, "You're so smart," or "Wow, I'm so proud of you," try using descriptive praise followed by, "You must be so proud of yourself."

"You picked up all the legos, trucks, and dolls and put them each in their bin. How organized! You must be so proud of yourself!"

CHAPTER 5

Power Struggles

Diffusing Power Struggles

Have you ever thought you'd be negotiating with a two or three year old; only to discover that you really can't reason with them?

Dad: "Lily, let's get dressed. It's time for bed."

Lily: "No"

Dad: "Here are your sleep undies; come on, put your legs in."

Lily: "No, I don't want those ones."

Dad (holding up a different pair): "Okay, how about these?"

Lily: "No, I don't like this one."

Dad (giving up): "Okay, fine, you pick which one."

Lily: "No. I don't want any."

After another 5 minutes of pointless negotiation, Dad got fed up, grabbed Lily, and put her sleep undies and pajamas on her while she screamed and flailed as hard as a twenty-month-old could.

She was finally dressed for bed. Victory for Dad! My husband could see the finish line.

But Lily had other plans. While screaming at the top of her lungs, she got undressed, took her sleep undies off, threw them down the stairs with a ferocious scream, and glared at Daddy.

It looks like Lily won that round, Dad.

There have been moments when I've been unable to handle one of my children's new behaviors and have cried tears of frustration and exhaustion. I know what it's like to constantly bang heads with someone when every interaction is laced with a bit of hesitancy or when you feel like you're walking on eggshells because you're unsure if you'll unleash the beast.

I was particularly tired of our constant disagreements about mundane but necessary tasks we always needed to do - like tidying up, taking a shower, and turning in for the night. It was a struggle to get them to listen and follow instructions.

Toddlers can resist and challenge you every step of the way. They seem to have an aversion to the word "no." And if they can't get what they want? Then they bring out the big guns and hold you hostage.

Mandy, mom of 4: "My three-year-old, Belle, walked into the kitchen this morning and informed me, "Mom, if you don't give me the iPad, I'm going to stay in the kitchen and bother you." I was beyond shocked! How dare she talk to me that way. I said no, of course, but she ignored me and grabbed the iPad. I get so tired of these battles."

Do you need fresh strategies to complete your usual routines with little conflict? Are you tired of constantly battling your child over trivial things, like which clothes to wear or what plate to use? Time outs aren't working, and you're unwilling to resort to threats and spanks, so what can you do?

From what I've seen, most advice out there doesn't consider the parent-child relationship. It's all about quick fixes, which may be beneficial in the short term but are unsustainable in the long run. We've already covered how important your "special time" or "one-on-one" time with your child is. That's the foundation for ending the power struggles.

The next pillar in reducing power struggles is greater communication. Chapter 4 has all the tips and tricks for that.

These two tools will help keep you in the yellow zone.

But what else can we do?

IDENTIFYING COMMON TRIGGERS FOR POWER STRUGGLES

Power struggles are big fights over who gets their way. When our children approach us with a "you're not the boss of me" attitude, we become bulls seeing a red flag.

We're overwhelmed with anger, and our thoughts are brimming with disbelief. "You're a toddler, for crying out loud! Just listen! You're not the boss here! Oh, you are soo not going to win this one." The funny thing is, the battle is no longer about the object of the fight but rather about who will get their way.

There are several tactics to prevent power battles with our children, but only some of them will work if we don't first understand what sets us off. Fighting fire with fire never works. If we want our kids to calm down, we must first calm ourselves. They will mirror our actions as we quickly navigate through different emotional states. We're leading by example again.

It is incredibly challenging to parent how we want to when triggered. In those moments, we are simply reacting. It's almost like a gut instinct, and we don't fully understand what we're feel beyond anger. But if we take a step back and assess the situation rationally, we may realize that our first response might be a bit over the top.

Where do our triggers come from?

Anger always has another feeling behind it. It's a secondary emotion; another emotion precedes it. Look past your anger and identify the other emotion that sparked it. Your kid's actions may bring up unpleasant associations or memories. These are your triggers. They are subconsciously igniting that fire of outrage and annoyance. Your child's behavior may also cause you to doubt your parenting skills or feel hopeless.

So, our response to our child's behavior has less to do with the behavior itself and more with our trouble processing these feelings.

I always had a more challenging time with Izzy's tantrums, whereas my husband had a more challenging time with Anthony's. The more I reflect on this, the more I realize that it has nothing to do with our kids but rather us adults. I could see a lot of myself in Izzy, the good and bad. When she would throw a tantrum over trivial materialistic things, I would get angry primarily because I would worry about certain unwanted traits that circulate in my family and my husband's.

When I came to that realization, I was unburdened. I was, therefore, able to disengage from the power struggles and help my daughter through her tough times, however trivial they were.

If we become more aware of our triggers, we will not only be able to improve our parenting skills but also our general health and happiness.

It can seem odd that feelings you experienced as a kid are now manifesting themselves in your adult life. You might have forgotten about them.

But let's assume that when you were younger, you knew you might be in "trouble" if you dared to challenge your parents' authority, so, when your child fights, your gut screams that it's time to stop this "disobedience," when, in fact, it is normal for a kid to challenge their parents.

Weeping, whining, and temper tantrums may also serve as triggers. People who were not permitted to express their unpleasant feelings or were always worried about keeping up with the right appearances as children often see them as triggers.

As a result, we find it challenging to handle our child's outbursts of emotion and attempt to stop them with threats and sheer will.

To identify our triggers, we must first become aware of when we are triggered.

Here are some common signs

- Sudden increase in your heart rate in reaction to your kid.
- Thinking, "How dare he do this."
- Thinking, "I wouldn't dream of doing this when I was a kid."
- Unable to allow your child some control.
- Unwilling to listen to your kid, "I don't need to pay attention to his words."

Reflect on the underlying cause of your anger and try to identify the feeling accompanying it. Be honest with yourself. These reactions were automatic and occurred without us being able to fully process them at the time, so you will need to do this when you've calmed down.

Once you acknowledge the other emotions accompanying your anger, you can start working through them. This process, recognizing your emotions and rationalizing your reactions, will do wonders for your self-control.

HANDLING YOUR TODDLER'S POWER STRUGGLES

There is only one way to end a power struggle in the heat of the moment - which is excellent news! Less to remember. On the other hand, there are many ways to prevent them from happening.

In the moment

Imagine you're having a huge argument and are all fired up about standing your ground and winning. You're determined to get your way no matter what. You've squared off against your counterpart, and you're ready to fight when suddenly, your adversary peacefully walks away.

You might feel deflated, a bit idiotic for attempting to fight this reasonable person, and even liberated from your anger.

The next time your child attempts to engage you in a power struggle, try saying something like this.

"Honey, I've already explained where I stand. I love you too much to keep arguing about this," and walk away.

It takes two to tango. Let go of the rope and watch the tug of war end.

Now, if your child is particularly stubborn, you might have to ignore whatever tantrum will come your way. The good news is that after a few times, your kid will learn that they will not be able to engage you in a power struggle and will stop trying.

Prevention is the best medicine -
Let's stay in the yellow zone.

At this age, toddlers are starting to realize that they have free will, and they are getting a sense of who they are. Although it may seem obvious to us, this is a fresh and intriguing notion to them, and they want to explore it.

It's like buying a new car and wanting to drive it around.

The result? Constantly putting our requests to the test, standing their ground, or flat-out refusing to comply.

For instance, "Stop banging on the table" might result in a concerto of bangs.

How do we save our ears and our sanity?

By allowing our children to make some decisions.

Offer your child a choice when there is not one.

Offering your child some control over situations when they may otherwise push back is a great way to encourage her growth and development.

Wearing a jacket is non-negotiable, so say, "Would you like to wear your red or yellow jacket?"

Teeth brushing? Also non-negotiable, say, "Would you like to brush your teeth before or after bath time today?"

"Would you like me to sing you a song or tell you a story before naptime?"

"Would you like to buckle yourself in your car seat, or would you like me to do it?"

If you need to up the ante, you can also add a time stressor.

"Would you like to buckle yourself in your car seat, or would you like me to do it? We're in a bit of a hurry, so I'll count to ten so you can know how much time you have to decide."

Make sure that you sound normal and non-threatening. Feel free to smile, too. It'll throw your kid off and save you from a power struggle.

A few of ground rules:

- Only offer two options. Anything more than that can overwhelm, cause hesitation, or fail to get cooperation.
- Don't provide her with options you don't want her to pick. You must be willing to accept and implement any of her options.
- Do not give them options for everything. You should only provide choices when they are necessary or relevant. If not, your toddler could believe she has a choice even when she doesn't or when it doesn't make sense to.

Relax, breathe, and give them space.

I want you to imagine what it would be like if you woke up every single day to someone telling you what to wear, what to eat, how much to eat, how to act, how to sit, how to play, what to play with, what time to go to bed, and much more.

You would go crazy. I know I would. I would start a huge rebellion and fight for control at every turn.

"Free will" is something we completely understand and accept for adults, yet we often forget that our children have some too and need to express it. They are unique individuals with their own thoughts, feelings, and experiences. Just because they are small doesn't mean that they don't have or need the same emotional freeness that we possess. We also want them to get used to expressing free will while in our care so that once they turn 18, they don't abuse their new freedom simply because they haven't had a chance to use it yet.

Our job is to determine what values we wish to pass on and how to teach those lessons. We did not copy and paste them into this world. They are not miniature replicas of us but rather individuals who will use what they learn from us to create their own identities.

Decide what to control and relax your grip on the little details. You and your child will be happier and healthier for it.

Let her wear mismatched clothes or a superhero cape to the grocery store or around the house, but stand your ground when it comes to your Sunday church attire.

Allow natural consequences to teach the lessons you can't.

There are times when you just can't win. In these cases, it's best to let your kid deal with the natural consequences independently.

Natural consequences are great at teaching children valuable lessons and making those lessons stick. The best part is that you won't have to do any yelling, nagging, or reminding.

If it is safe for them to learn the consequence naturally, then generally speaking, you should allow it to happen. Going out in the cold without a jacket might be okay, but running out onto a busy street is most certainly not.

Pitfall: Don't use "I told you so" or over-explain the consequences. They most likely understood the consequence on their own. If not, try asking probing questions instead of saying, "I told you so" or lecturing.

Solve problems together.

If you and your toddler keep butting heads over the same issue, then it's time for some good old-fashioned problem-solving. Find a moment when everyone is relaxed, grab a pen and paper, and problem solve together. Use the format discussed in the previous chapter.

Be willing to listen if they have an issue with your suggestions. Giving them a voice, relaxing over the little details, learning from their mistakes, and working through issues with them are all important things we can do as teachers. If the solution you guys decided on is not working, go back to the drawing board until you can come up with one that does.

Make someone else the boss.

You can sometimes remove yourself from the fight and make someone or something else the boss.

"The dentist called and said that we must brush our teeth before bed so we don't get cavities." Feel free to use visual aids to show what a cavity is and get them more interested in the task.

Routine charts are a great way to establish a morning and bedtime routine without nagging your child through it. Check out our routine examples on our website.

Instead of, "Come on, it's time to brush our teeth. Let's go! Move it!" try, "Oh, looks like you're showered and have your pajamas on! Wonderful! What's next on your checklist?"

BUILDING A PEACEFUL HOME

New parents always talk about baby-proofing their homes. You can get cupboard locks, door knob locks, and corner covers for the sharp tables, and the list goes on and on. But no one ever talks about toddler proofing your home.

You know that "my house is too quiet feeling"? It's almost instantly followed by dread.

One day, I was distracted in the kitchen when I noticed Lily had been abnormally quiet. I was about to start looking for her when she came bouncing down the stairs, exclaiming, "Mom! I put shampoo in my hair." I remember thinking, "Wow, that's a lot of shampoo, but at least she put it where it was supposed to go." I rushed her to the tub and began rinsing her hair out, only to realize that it was not shampoo that she'd lathered in there. After a quick scan of the area, I noticed a tub of petroleum jelly on the floor. Ahh!! She'd put an entire tub of petroleum jelly in her hair!

And I had now spread it all over her hair while trying to rinse it. It took five washes with castile soap, three washes with Dawn dish soap, a three-hour tapioca flour soak, and another two washes with shampoo to get her hair to just look "I'm dirty" greasy rather than "I love petroleum jelly too much" greasy!

Yes, my house and my sanity both need protection from Lily. And Lily needs to have the freedom to roam the house without being constantly followed, chastised, or the object of my annoyance.

Speaking of annoyance, since becoming a mother, I've come to appreciate the profound impact that one's home has on one's emotional well-being.

Are you feeling on edge, short-tempered, or stressed? Check your environment to determine whether it's making things worse. Dirty dishes, crumbs all over the floor, piles of laundry… seeing these messes will not help your stress levels.

Fortunately, all it takes are a few easy adjustments and new routines to transform your space into the serene haven you've always imagined it to be.

We are trying to achieve two things with this transformation. The first, of course, is to toddler-proof our home in order to reduce the power struggles. The second is to create a decision-rich environment where our little toddlers can feel important and can contribute to our family.

Toddler proofing

Make a list of all the things in your home that make you want to pull your hair out.

For example:

- Climbing on counters
- Getting into toiletries

- Pulling clothes off hangers
- Raiding the pantry
- Raiding the fridge

Most of the issues can be solved with a few well-placed child locks, thus allowing us to control the environment. We have not, however, created a decision-rich environment, a pivotal element in reducing power struggles.

Toddlers need to feel like they possess some form of control and power. There are endless ways of empowering them. Here are a few examples to get your creative juices flowing:

- Relocate cups, plates, and bowls to a bottom cupboard to allow toddlers to get themselves some water or set the table.
- Install a secondary hanging closet rod where you can place a few outfits for your toddler to pick out their own clothes.
- Put in a low-level hook in the bedroom so your toddler can hang his pajamas or other items of clothing that can be worn again.
- Have a few well-placed step stools - in front of the bathroom sink or by the kitchen counter/sink, allowing your toddler to wash their hands or participate in cooking.
- Place some healthy snack options on the bottom shelves of the cupboards and the fridge for a help-yourself snack option.
- Have an accessible shoe rack to teach your tot to get ready on his own and return his shoes when he comes home.
- Place a big basket or a low set of hooks by the door with coats and winter gear.

- Enlist your children in participating in family contributions, a.k.a. chores. A few fun ones are vacuuming, washing pots and pans, washing the car, watering the plants, spraying the windows and walls, and wiping them.

These are just a few examples of how you can empower and make your toddler feel independent at home and, therefore, less likely to fight you for control and power. Tailor these suggestions to your home and develop a few additional options.

It is important to note that you will need to take time to train your children and show them how to care for themselves. You know your child best; try to identify areas causing issues, and brainstorm solutions that promote independence.

Declutter all surfaces/childproof your home

Clutter in our visual environment is one of the leading causes of mental chaos. Just like how a cluttered environment would affect your stress levels, the same goes for your children.

Include your child in the process of decluttering your home. This should take 30 minutes. Schedule a time daily or weekly when the family cleans together. Play a cleanup song or other music, and set a timer. Either work with your child or assign them an independent task of their choosing.

After decluttering your space, the challenge lies in maintaining a consistently clean house, especially with young children. Toddlers are notorious for making huge messes within a short time.

However, by controlling the environment, you can reduce the number of things your toddler can get into and, thus, the number of messes created.

Let's talk about your toddlers' space

Just like you need your own space untouched by the kids, the kids need their space where they can feel free to explore their environment without constant supervision.

Consider establishing a designated play area within your home. This technique confines the toy mess to a single room; facilitating quicker cleanup and preventing children from playing right under your feet as you cook or clean. Transform a section of the living room or utilize a spare room as a playroom.

When we moved into a smaller home, the garage was the only space we could convert into a playroom. We covered everything we didn't want them to touch by hanging old bed sheets from the ceiling as dividers. Out of sight, out of mind. The kids love being in there, especially since it is close to the kitchen. They feel the security of having mom nearby while enjoying the big play space.

Beware of cluttering the play space with too many toys. Less is more, especially when it comes to toys. Surround your child with toys that promote imaginary play and toys with multiple functions - such as legos or blocks - rather than a one-dimensional play option.

You know the feeling when you find something that you haven't used in a while, and suddenly, it feels brand new? This is a great tool to use with toys.

Start a toy rotation. Whenever you notice that your toddler hasn't touched a particular toy in a few days, hide the toy and bring a different one out. After a few weeks, the same will happen with the new toy and you can rotate through the toys again.

If you want your child to be able to pick between trains, blocks, and legos rather than have only one of the three accessible at any given time, then consider organizing and categorizing them in baskets, buckets, and cabinets. If your children aren't reading yet, use visual cues such as pictures taped to the relevant containers. Children who know where to find a certain toy are less likely to scatter everything while searching.

Furthermore, instilling a sense of responsibility in your children by encouraging them to participate in the cleaning process is essential. Establish consistent rules that must be followed daily, such as tidying up toys before dinnertime and storing books before bedtime. When cleanup is part of your routine, children are more inclined to clean up regularly. This can be part of your daily thirty minutes of cleaning or just a separate step in your bedtime routine.

If you are having a hard time getting your kids to clean up, they might have too many toys. Reduce the number of toys your children have and only allow them to take one toy out at a time. They must pack up the previous toy before taking a new one out. The cleanup process then becomes much easier and more manageable, making it exponentially more likely that the kids will participate and consistently clean up.

Remember to use descriptive commands and praises when encouraging cleaning up.

Put everything where it belongs

There should be a place for everything in your house. This little trick has made a huge difference for me. When something does not have a home, I either find one for it or discard it.

Put clothing away in drawers or the closet, store food in the fridge or pantry, place shoes in their cubbies, collect dirty clothes in the laundry basket, place cups in the sink, and place dirty dishes in the dishwasher rather than leaving them out.

This helps establish order and encourages the early development of responsibility in young children.

If you show kids where things belong, they can help you put them there. Starting young with these habits ensures that they will last well into adulthood - your child's future spouse will thank you for that.

Also, when they help clean up, you won't have to follow after them as much since they already know where everything goes. If kids resist, make it a game. "Let's beat the timer!" You can also think of the fun aspect of chores from a child's perspective, like button pushing, touching water, or using an appliance.

"Once we've loaded all the clothes in the dishwasher, then you can throw the soap in and push the button to start it." "When you've picked up all your toys off the floor, then you can vacuum."

CHAPTER 6

Tantrums

Tiptoeing The Tantrum Train

Dad: "Hey, champ, we need to put on our clothes so that we can go to Grandma's house."

Bo, age 3: "I really, really want to go to Grandma's!"

Dad: "I know, buddy. Let's get dressed first."

Bo: "No!"

Dad: "We can't leave the house without clothes on, kiddo."

Bo (crying and protesting): "Noo! I don't want to get dressed!"

At this point, I can guarantee you two things: the first, they were late to Grandma's, and the second, Dad wished he had a magical teleportation device to get him out of earshot.

As a parent, I have experienced the confounding nature of limit-pushing behavior firsthand. It can be perplexing and frustrating when our sweet little darlings throw tantrums at us when we ask them to do something reasonable or appropriate. I mean, what's wrong with putting clothes on?

I remember a phase we went through with my oldest daughter, Izzy, when she was about three and a half years old. Every morning, we would have an hour's long tantrum. First, she wanted to hold hands as she walked down the stairs. Next, she wanted to eat from the pink bowl, not the white bowl. Then it would be which chair to sit on, what water cup to drink from, etc. The requests were endless. And they were very, very specific. One small misstep and then the small tantrum would turn into full-blown rage.

The problem for me wasn't the requests themselves, though that was annoying, but rather the whiny tone of voice and tears with which they were delivered. It would drive me mad, especially since I was exhausted with a new baby and barely awake when they started.

Was she trying to test the limits of my patience?

Why couldn't she just ask nicely?

Does she get a kick out of seeing me frustrated and angry?

And after about the fourth request, boy, would I get angry. It was tough to keep my cool while my blood was boiling. Overtired mom and whiny toddler are not a good combination. My mantra keeping me from hulk mode became, "She's only 3, she's only 3; get food in that belly, and it'll all be better."

While challenging, it's important to remember that these behaviors are a normal part of their development and growth. It's our role as parents to navigate these moments with understanding and patience, and teach our little ones how to handle their big emotions.

How do we do that?

Remember the mirroring effect we talked about earlier? The quickest and best way for them to learn how to handle themselves when their emotions are high is by watching you, the parent, handle yourself when your emotions are high.

So, as much as I felt like screaming, throwing, punching, or scolding with my brewing anger, I knew I couldn't. I had in the past, and the consequences were embarrassingly displayed back to me when Izzy would huff dramatically at her siblings or yell at them or threaten them with ultimatums or, to my utmost dismay, say, "I spanked Lily's butt because she wasn't being a good listener."

I could see all of my reactions in her, and I did not like it one bit.

So I needed to do better. I needed to make sure that I was in the best position possible to handle myself when emotions were raging - which goes back to taking care of myself.

I remember from childhood when my father would scold my older brother, saying he was setting the example for us younger siblings. But in reality, the example was already set by him, the father.

We'll dive into strategies to keep calm later in this chapter.

But first, What is a tantrum?

A temper tantrum is a sudden outburst of strong emotions, such as rage, grief, loss, disappointment, or extreme frustration.

This emotional outburst in toddlers around the age of 2 may cause them to weep, thrash, scream, strike their parents, tumble, kick, bite, hurl items, hit their heads, or hold their breath.

The ages between two and four are known as the "terrible twos", "trying threes", and the "ferocious fours" for good reasons.

I remember vividly when "the terrible twos" started in my house. My oldest daughter entered that faze around eighteen months, her twin brother around two years of age, and eight months later, my third daughter began her temper tantrums. It felt endless. Between the screaming, crying, and whining, it felt like I was hit by an emotional tsunami for a couple of years.

I constantly walked on eggshells, never knowing when the tantrum express would take off. I was anxious, stressed, and clueless about how to deal with them.

I remember my tantrum lightbulb moment. My husband was being particularly snippy one day. He was complaining and grumbling all afternoon. Just out of reflex, I said, "Would you quit your tantrum?" He looked at me angrily and replied, "Well, I'm tired and hungry!"

Fireworks went off in my brain.

Is that what it was like for my kids? Were they feeling these big things in their bodies and brains but just couldn't figure out how to let those feelings out (express them) and deal with them?

Temper tantrums fall into two categories: emotional meltdowns and non-emotional tantrums, often known as Little Nero tantrums.

The non-emotional, Little Nero, tantrums are the ones that are on purpose to manipulate you, the adult, into giving in. The child is entirely in control of their emotions and is choosing this path to reach their goal.

Why? Simple, because it has worked in the past.

> Michaela - mom of 2 - "My daughter Mila (4) is with her dad during the week and with me on the weekend. Her dad wants to be the favorite parent, so anytime she whines for something, he immediately gives it to her. She now will throw a tantrum and whine nonstop to get her way."

I have experienced this firsthand with my children. There are times when I've felt exhausted, overwhelmed, or just fed up! In those moments, I've given in to their tantrums just so I could get a minute of peace and quiet.

And that's precisely what I got.

A minute.

It wasn't too long after I would give in that the next whine episode would start.

Giving in taught the little kiddos a few things:

- Perseverance - "If I just keep going long enough, she'll give in."
- Observational skills - "When I hit this high note or make these repetitive squeals, she gives in instantly."
- Deduction powers - "I can do this for absolutely everything I want!"

I'm sure you'd agree that there are better ways of learning these life skills. As soon as I figured out their game, I doubled down on the Little Nero tantrums.

Here's how I handle them now.

"Honey, I can see that you're upset and really wanted to have another cupcake (true story as I type this); the problem is if you eat two cupcakes, you won't be hungry for lunch, and we won't have any for tomorrow's snack. Would you like to sit next to me and color as I work, or go downstairs and keep playing?"

The recipe = acknowledge feeling + the problem (state the real problem, not some made-up issue about fairies and bunnies) + offer an alternative option if applicable.

If you're lucky, that'll be the end of it. If not, you'll have to break out your secret power: ignore, stay calm, and carry on. I've got some tips later in the chapter to help you through this highly stressful time.

Now, let's talk about the real/uncontrollable tantrums. These emotional meltdowns occur when the emotional part of the brain (limbic) becomes overstimulated and seizes control from the reasoning portion of the brain (prefrontal cortex). It seems to be contagious among all youngsters. (If you have more than one little one, you'll get what I mean.)

Two and three-year-olds lack the cognitive ability to reason or manipulate. When they're agitated, they often have emotional toddler meltdowns.

Even older kids and adults sometimes have emotional breakdowns (just like my husband did). The difference is that toddlers don't have the know-how to calm themselves down.

A child who throws a temper tantrum is not necessarily misbehaving or defiant. After all, they just figured out how to sit, crawl, walk, eat, play, and so much more. They're not trying to "be bad" (and I put that in quotation because no child is bad). When they throw emotional fits and refuse to stop sobbing, they tell us that they are experiencing emotional distress and cannot handle it on their own.

They need our help.

The importance of investigating tantrum causes

Let me start by saying no tantrum is without cause. It's basic physics. Action causes reaction. The cause might not be reasonable to you, the adult, but honestly, it doesn't need to be. Your toddler lives in the world of teddy bears, trains, and pretend play, not the world of mortgages, bills, and work. Their problems are not your problems, nor should they be. They will throw tantrums if they have a kid reason, not an adult one.

I want you to think of your child as a hot air balloon. If the balloon is properly cared for, it will soar in the sky, and you are in the sunny, happy yellow zone. If your balloon is carrying some sandbags, then it's struggling to stay up, and it's in the orange. The red zone comes in when there are way too many sandbags that you can't seem to untie and throw overboard, and your balloon is about to crash.

So to keep the balloon up in the air (your child happy and tantrum-free), we need to ensure the hot air balloon is sandbag-free.

What are the sandbags? Some are physical, and some are emotional.

THE PHYSICAL SANDBAGS

We've already covered meeting physical needs in Chapter 2, so here's a quick recap.

Your toddler needs to eat.

Ever notice how cranky your little one can get right before meal times? Or maybe the sudden burst of happy energy after the meal? A hungry belly can cause quite a big ruckus.

Your toddler needs sleep.

We went through a phase where we thought our oldest daughter Izzy was done with naps because she refused to go down when the time came. We paid for that mistake with a string of wild tantrums for a couple months until we finally figured it out.

Toddlers have a difficult time expressing their exhaustion, which results in temper tantrums. Some signs of overtiredness are:

- Irritability
- Sluggishness
- Refusal to participate in any activities
- Uncooperativeness

Your toddler needs to use the bathroom.

Some toddlers can feel the urge in their bodies and need help identifying what it is and dealing with it, especially with belly aches that accompany constipation. They are feeling something in their body and can't quite express it. Explain it to them and help them get to the bathroom.

Your toddler is not feeling well.

I could probably count the days my kids weren't sick in the last month quicker than the days they were. Toddlers are sick nonstop. Especially if they attend daycare or have frequent playdates outside the house. We all need a little extra TLC when we're sick, more so if you're a little tiny human.

THE EMOTIONAL SANDBAGS

Your kid is trying to get your attention.

At that precious young age, our kids love us, parents, so much. We are at the center of their universe. They would love nothing more than our undivided attention and to spend the whole day playing with us. In fact, they need our attention to thrive. If they don't get our attention positively, they will get it negatively.

Introducing the attention-seeking tantrum. It's the first alarm that your toddler needs more attention. Their behavior will keep escalating if they don't get what they need. So you can consider this a warning shot, so to speak.

Your toddler is overstimulated.

Overstimulation can occur when kids are swamped by more noises, experiences, sensations, and activities than they can cope with. It can lead to stress, frustration, and discomfort for the child, especially if they already struggle to cope with the sensory overload.

I used to believe that overstimulation was mostly due to technology. And in this modern era, it is. We got rid of our TV when we had our first kids (you're either thinking, "That's so extreme," or, "Awesome I want to do that"). My husband championed this decision. He studied human development and family studies with his degree in communication. He pointed out the plethora of research that explains how technology harms children, especially in those first few years, that are crucial to their development. We saw the tantrums firsthand with nieces and nephews and with our children in the rare instances they did get access to an iPad.

But technology is not the only reason for an overstimulation tantrum.

Overstimulation can come from too many toys jam-packed in a messy toy room.

> Marie, mom of 4: "I have a basement full of toys, more toys than you can ever dream of. I have to nag and nag them to go play with their toys and leave me alone. Do they play down there? Sometimes. But they're always crabby. It makes me feel like they don't appreciate all their stuff."

I experienced this, too, with my children. I always thought, "If they just had this one toy, then they'll go play and leave me alone for a bit." What seems like a thousand toys later, and I still haven't found the so-called one magic toy.

A family friend, who also happened to be a retired Waldorf teacher, called me up once and said, "I want to come over and help you design play spaces for your children." I remember thinking, "Really? They need a designer for a play space?" I did not want to be rude, so I allowed this experiment to happen.

Imagine my surprise when she told me to get rid of 90 percent of their toys and that I was overstimulating them with the bright rug and all the "extra and unnecessary stuff." With her guidance, I set up a Montessori-style playroom. The kids started spending their days in their new toy room without a prompt. It's a calm space filled with wooden toys and soothing colors. It makes them feel relaxed and confident to be alone and explore.

Overstimulation can also occur in big social settings. "We just had a wonderful time at your friend's party. Why are you crying?" It baffles us adults. They just had a blast; what do they have to be upset about? Nothing. Their bodies are just trying to catch up with all the activity around them.

A tantrum due to overstimulation can be cured with quiet time with a parent. Help them recenter themselves with a soothing activity, some cuddles, or reading, and offer your presence to solidify their sense of security.

Your kid is upset.

This sandbag is probably the easiest to identify. Broken toys, sibling fights, or stubbing a toe are but a few reasons to be upset. I'm sure you'd agree when I say that toddlers can find some of the most trivial things very upsetting.

There are times when you, the parent, are the reason your child is upset. They may be throwing a tantrum because you refused to give them a toy or said no to ice cream before dinner.

Simply acknowledge the child's feelings and ignore the tantrum. "It's upsetting when you can't get ice cream when you want it." "Boy, you really want some ice cream. The problem is, ice cream is not on the menu for dinner." "Ice Cream is so yummy, my favorite flavor is chocolate. Maybe we'll have an ice cream cake for my birthday."

Acknowledging the feeling doesn't mean you are giving in. Yes, ice cream is delicious. It doesn't mean you have to give it to them right this second. You can allow the fantasy, not the reality.

You may safely ignore your kid after acknowledging their feelings. The episode will end as soon as they focus on something else.

When Should I Worry About My Toddler's Tantrums

Temper tantrums are a natural and healthy aspect of growth. In rare cases, a toddler's tantrum may indicate an underlying condition.

If your child's tantrums are frequent, intense, and difficult to calm, there may be a deeper problem. In those extreme cases, tantrums could indicate that your child is experiencing mental health or cognitive-related issues such as anxiety, autism, mood disorders, ADHD, etc. If you have any concerns that your child may be dealing with one of these conditions or that their tantrums are atypical, please consult their doctor, a therapist, or a child psychologist for evaluation and resources.

PREVENT TEMPER TANTRUMS BEFORE THEY APPEAR

Prevention.

We've all heard the classic saying: prevention is the best medicine. It is no different in this case.

One approach that has worked for me is looking out for the HALT signs: H for hunger, A for anger, L for loneliness, and T for tired.

We've gone over, but it's worth repeating: kids are likelier to act out when hungry or worn out.

If any of the above factors are present, even the slightest trigger, like the wrong-colored cup, can ignite a tantrum. Therefore, establish a daily sleep, eating, and rest routine to avoid these tantrum pitfalls.

Boredom, tension, anger, frustration, or disappointment are all classic tantrum triggers (as discussed previously in this chapter).

Try to predict when meltdowns might happen and prevent them from occurring in the first place.

If you know that your kid will throw a tantrum when it's time to leave the playground, then be prepared and think of alternatives or diversions. A snack on the car ride home, perhaps? Or playing their favorite songs in the car?

For example, Izzy will typically wake up cranky from naps. I now know that when she wakes up, I'll need to spend 10 to 15 minutes rocking her, doing a calm activity, or giving her a snack right away. Those 15 minutes saved me from an hour of crying and whining.

It's far simpler to tap into their rationality to stop temper tantrums before they start than to stop them after they have already begun.

PRACTICAL STRATEGIES FOR STAYING CALM YOURSELF - IT STARTS WITH YOU

I can freely admit that temper tantrums used to put me in a state of mild terror, especially if they were in public. My heartbeat would get faster as I felt everyone's judging eyes on me. I would attempt to think quickly and devise a distraction for the child to stop the tantrum in its tracks. It rarely succeeded.

Children have an uncanny ability to pick up on our tension and anxiety, which only exacerbates the tantrum.

It gives them the message that their strong emotions are too much for us to handle, which is obviously not very reassuring.

You need to maintain your composure to help a child through a temper tantrum. They can sense your soothing presence even if they are yelling too loudly to hear you or if they are facing away from you and can't see you.

But how do we parents stay calm and keep our cool when our toddlers are beyond reason, making sometimes unrealistic demands and screaming their heads off?

Set yourself up for success

Take care of yourself daily and make sure you're getting enough "me-time." This will put you in the best position to tackle high-stress moments.

Change your mindset

When I finally understood that tantrums were just a way of releasing pent-up feelings and that I shouldn't stop anyone, let alone my child, from expressing those feelings, then a mindset shift happened. I could let go of the sense that I need to "stop" tantrums midstream. I was finally able to breathe a bit better. The release of tension enabled me to remain calm, which, in turn, hastened the end of the tantrum. We can influence many things in a young kid's life, but we cannot change how they feel.

I am no longer the "tantrum police" but rather a guide that helps my kids through their intense emotions.

My job is to allow the expression of feelings and offer empathy and understanding, especially when I don't agree.

Allow extra minutes.

Start tasks early, and give yourself extra minutes. Worst case scenario, a tantrum happens, and you have a few additional minutes to deal with it without getting stressed and rushing to finish a task or get somewhere on time. Best case scenario, everything goes smoothly, and you can have a few extra minutes to cuddle your little one and give them some positive attention.

Reduce wordiness.

Anyone can go insane trying to have a conversation with a wailing toddler. Do not try to teach a lesson, bargain, or use logic when the tantrum is in full force. It is not the right time. A youngster who is yelling inconsolably isn't going to listen to you for two reasons:

- His emotions and screams are very loud
- He is not in his right mind

After your kid has calmed down (which he will, I promise), you can calmly sit and discuss the outburst.

Create a safe haven - physically and mentally

If you feel yourself losing your grip and can't stay calm, consider stepping away to a quiet space and regroup. (As long as you know your child or children will be safe from harm). This trick is good for two reasons:

- You are modeling an appropriate way to deal with strong emotions.
- You're actually taking a break and, hopefully will be able to calm down.

Simply state, "I'm feeling angry and frustrated; I'm going to go to my room and calm down," and walk away. Close the door if you need to, and take a couple of minutes.

If you cannot physically remove yourself from your child's presence, try putting an earbud into your ear and tuning in on your favorite podcast or a good parenting book. Anything that involves stimulating adult conversation to help you regain perspective and calmness.

IN THE MOMENT

Tantrums are no walk in the park. I'd like to equip you with some classic terrorist negotiation tactics for de-escalation and preserving your sanity.

Don't use the word "no".

Using "no" or trying to reason with a youngster who is having a tantrum will not work. The toddler's brain switches to "survival mode" after a breakdown. It turns off the rational portion of the brain and responds instinctively to danger, regardless of its veracity. If the reasoning portion of our brains were working under actual danger, we could pause or attempt to use logic, which might endanger our lives. This is a classic case of the "fight or flight" survival response. When a kid is having a breakdown, it is common for the so-called alarm to go off even when there is no real danger. It's like installing a burglar alarm on your roof only to find that it goes off every time a bird lands on it. For this reason, while the hindbrain is in charge, it's best to be quiet and play it safe until the forebrain can take over again. Setting limits, telling your kid "no," and disciplining them are all things you should do, but if you want those actions to genuinely help your child, you must wait until the forebrain is in charge.

Watch your tone.

The more you tell your kid to "stop," "calm down," or "snap out of it," the less likely you are to get them to do any of those things. It makes no difference how assertively or politely you ask. Put a temporary pause on all of your other expectations.

Don't shout to be heard above your child's screams.

Shouting makes you seem aggressive and does little to calm a volatile situation. It's critical to realize that your child's brain sees danger when the fight-or-flight response kicks in. They need to know that everything will be okay and not feel threatened by screams.

You may say, "My kid knows I wouldn't hurt them." Without a doubt, they do. However, your youngster is not thinking rationally in these instances. Their brain responds automatically, so anything that seems scary will worsen the problem.

Accept their emotions, but not their behavior.

Everyone has the right to feel the way they do about anything. Imagine telling your friend that you're having a tough time at work. They respond, "Oh, suck it up; it's just work," or maybe, "I have it worse - my boss is so mean," or perhaps, "Oh, you poor thing - you should just quit and find a nice comfy job that's easier." You might feel unheard, annoyed, or incapable. What if your friend responded with, "That sounds like a tough situation." How would you feel then? Calmer, relieved at being heard and understood, connected to the person who simply acknowledged how you feel. By acknowledging your child's emotions, you're showing that you value and respect their inner world.

Many of the parents I speak with believe that just because you are acknowledging the emotion, you are allowing the act that follows. That is simply not true.

Emotion and Action are separate things. And that is precisely what we are trying to teach our toddlers.

We can't help but feel our emotions, but our actions, we can control.

"You are feeling upset because you got the blue cup, and you wanted the purple one instead." Or, "You're feeling frustrated because the block tower keeps falling."

Warning! Avoid using "but." Anything said before a "but" becomes completely irrelevant. When acknowledging their feelings, use "because" instead of "but" or any other negative sequence connectors. This technique is known as emotional coaching.

Give them their space.

Everyone has their own personal "bubble," but when emotions get big, the bubbles need to get big, too. How would you feel if someone tried to hug you when your blood was boiling with anger?

If your kid doesn't ask, stay at least three feet away from them. If they are not in danger, avoid attempting to hug or carry them. When they're already overwhelmed by intense emotions, feeling confined or locked in may make the situation much worse. If you aren't sure, you can ask them, "Would you like a hug?" Crouch down, hold your hands open, and wait for them to come when they're ready.

Watch your facial expressions and body language.

Maintain a relaxed, collected demeanor throughout your child's tantrum. The easiest way to achieve this is to pay attention to your facial expressions and body language. Maintain a neutral look on your face. Check if you're clenching your jaw, frowning, or making other negative facial expressions.

Be deliberate with your body language as well. Avoid placing your hands on your hips or crossing your arms. Do not make sweeping movements with your hands or pace back and forth.

Drop down to your kid's eye level.

Don't look down on, or stand over them while you converse. It projects an air of dominance, which is counterproductive during a meltdown. It might also make them feel unsafe or challenged.

Sit with your kid, if they will. If not, kneel so you can talk to them face-to-face (although it's usually best to talk as little as possible during a tantrum). Keep your hands in a natural, forward stance in front of your body.

Don't engage in power struggles.

Your toddler will sometimes refuse to do things simply because you are the one telling them to. They're exerting their newfound power to say "no". The thing is, you're far better off not engaging at all. You can say, "I love you and don't want to argue with you," and walk away. You're letting go of the rope; therefore, you're still standing, untouched and untroubled by all the pushback your little one is trying to throw at you. It's a powerful shift in perspective that has helped me navigate these challenging moments.

Do not be insistent.

The overload of demands is sometimes the root cause of the breakdown. But no matter what's happening, you should avoid making more demands when things are out of control.

Draw them out.

There are times when you've acknowledged their feelings, but your tot can't seem to shake the tantrum or sobs. They haven't quite mastered the art of calming down yet. You can help them get there by starting the calm-down activity and letting them take over once they are capable:

- Sing or hum a calming tune
- Start a coloring or painting project
- Sit down with a book
- Get on the ground and do some stretches and breathing
- Puzzles
- Any quiet activity

Once your child has calmed down, allow them to take over the activity. Later, when he's back to his usual self, say, "The coloring helped you calm down, you can come color anytime you need to."

CHAPTER 7

Aggressive Behavior

The Little Tysons

Little Anthony started a new toddler phase. He decided to give himself an excuse to hit, bite, and pinch. "I'm a monster! Rarrr!" he screams, chasing his sisters around the house, biting them, and pinching his baby brother's cheeks. I'm sure you can imagine my rage and frustration. Why can't he pretend to be a nice monster or better yet a flower or a monkey?!

There's nothing quite as scary and enraging as your child being aggressive. In my experience, these are the moments where it's hardest to practice self-control and battle those knee-jerk reactions.

"I just want to nip this in the bud" or "How dare he hit his sister!" are just a few thoughts that might accompany those quick reactions that almost always result in us responding aggressively. An aggressive grab, smack on the butt, timeout, yelling, taking away toys... we're so busy focusing on how angry, frustrated, or scared we are feeling that we completely miss the root of the problem and, therefore, solution.

In this "I'm a monster" example, Anthony was thriving on the attention hits he was getting from all his aggressive behavior. After all, every time he bit or hit a sibling I, or any other adult around, would stop everything to deal with him and, as a result, be present to him. It's not like I can just ignore him when he's hurting others.

However, negative attention is not the sole reason for aggressive behavior, especially for younger toddlers. Since they are still in the early stages of language development, toddlers primarily depend on their behaviors to "inform" us what they are feeling or thinking. You may find that your toddler "talks" with his movements rather than with words. Instead of saying, "Mommy, I want to play with that toy," he might take your hand, lead you to the toy shelf, and point to the one he wants.

In times of rage, frustration, exhaustion, or overload, toddlers might resort to physical means (such as punching, shoving, slapping, grabbing, kicking, or biting) to convey their message:

"I'm upset! You're invading my personal space; back off!"

"I'm in overdrive and need help to slow down."

"I envy what you have and want it for myself."

Simply put, sometimes aggressive behavior in toddlers is just their way of communicating.

One of our primary responsibilities as parents is to teach our children to identify and express their emotions in healthy, constructive ways.

This is by no means an easy job. Sometimes, as adults, we struggle to recognize and express our emotions. It takes a lot of effort and endurance. But with your guidance and as you take on your role as a teacher, your kid will learn.

UNDERSTANDING THE CAUSES OF AGGRESSIVE BEHAVIOR

There is always a cause for any behavior. Aggressiveness is no different. By understanding the cause, then we can focus on the appropriate solution. When kids are aggressive, it indicates various underlying issues falling under these three categories: physical problems, life situations (a.k.a. emotional problems), and mental illnesses.

So, the first step in handling violence is to figure out why it's happening. Let's rule out mental illnesses before we dive into this chapter.

1- Mental Illness

If you feel your child is displaying excessive behaviors of aggression, impulsivity, or explosive emotional outbursts, and you suspect your child may have a mental disorder, contact your pediatrician or seek out a mental health professional to assess your child. Some children may need more support than others, and asking for professional help is okay.

2- Physical Problems

We've already touched upon in Chapter 2 how important it is to meet our children's physical needs. Kids will lash out when hungry, tired, in pain, or if they haven't had enough outdoor time. If those needs aren't met positively, they will lash out and find a way to get them met negatively.

When Anthony came home from surgery, he felt a fair bit of pain and discomfort. He was terrorizing his sisters, hitting and biting them. He was on pain meds for a couple of days. I started noticing a pattern between the timing of his aggressiveness and his doses of pain meds. The hitting would start whenever it was nearing the time of another dose of meds. He was in pain and lashed out at others.

Just because I understood why he was lashing out does not mean I accepted the behavior. It means I can relate to him better and, therefore, reach and reason with him.

Toddlers also need to get out of the house and release some energy. Dr. Claire McCarthy from Harvard Health Publishing says children need an hour of outdoor time daily. I advocate for more than that. Sun exposure and getting enough vitamin D, are extremely important to our children. Vitamin D is a massive benefactor to our physical and emotional health. If your children don't have free access to a backyard, consider adding a couple of walks into your daily schedule.

3- Life Situations Stressor

Life situation stressors are simply things that happen outside our control. It is - essentially - change. Kids do not react well to change because it disrupts their predictable pattern, thus their security blanket.

Does this mean that we should avoid change like the plague? Well, no. That's not how life works, and we do want our kids to learn how to adapt to change quickly and in a healthy way. It's an important life skill. Our job is to assist them in navigating the change while ensuring that their emotional and physical needs are still met. In my experience, change is also when we drop the ball on parenting since we get overloaded with other tasks.

We often hear the term regression when big life events happen, like a new sibling being born, moving houses, starting preschool, the death of a loved one, etc. Regressions can come in all shapes and forms. For example, when my fourth baby was born, Lily went through a big speech regression, Izzy had explosive fits of rage, and luckily, Anthony would just sneak away from whoever was watching him and glue himself to my hip.

In my experience, regression is simply a lack of needs being met. Once you pinpoint those needs and meet them in positive ways, the regression stops.

IMMEDIATE STRATEGIES FOR
PREVENTING AGGRESSION IN TODDLERS

I have read so many parenting books that skid around or vaguely explain what to do when toddlers get aggressive. If there is ever a time for clear step-by-step instructions, then it is now. I do not want to leave you with more questions or confusion, so I'll make this as plain as possible.

I can see my toddler hitting. I'm angry, embarrassed, frustrated! What should I do?

You're angry, and your toddler is angry. Tensions are high, and it would only take one little push for this battle to become a war. Now is not the time to impart life lessons, teach your kid a new skill, or make them understand the error of their ways.

Let's try to relate. If you're angry and ready to hit, how would you feel if someone walked up to you and started preaching? You'd most likely get even more enraged and want to shove them away from you, no matter how right they are.

When we approach our out-of-control toddler with more physical or verbal aggression, two things will likely happen.

The first would be a repeat of the unwanted behavior, either out of spite or for another negative attention hit, and the second would be a severe blow to your child's self-esteem. "Mom said I'm mean; it must be true.", "I guess she's not busy anymore when I pull Kelly's hair. Kelly is her favorite."

We want to teach our children that violence is unacceptable without labeling or berating them. After all, we wouldn't tell our kids they suck at math if they failed one assignment. No, we'd want them to keep working hard and try again.

Remember the mirroring effect we talked about? Managing your anger and frustration healthily is important since your children learn by watching you.

That being said, I don't want you to smile at your kid if he pushes his brother, hurts his friend, or starts throwing toys around. So what to do?

Step 1 - Stay Calm

This first step is the most important and, quite honestly, the hardest. In these very intense, aggressive moments, you only have a split second to calm yourself before engaging your child. Your child is more likely to relax if you maintain composure. The angrier you react to your child's tantrum, the angrier your toddler will become.

When our toddlers are "losing it," they need our presence to be a steady anchor.

Step 2 - End the Aggression

Any hostile behavior needs instant intervention. Give no reminders or cautions to cease; step in and end the aggression. Walk right up to them, crouch down, and get their attention. A simple, loud "Hey!" might do the trick; if it doesn't, then pick one of them up and take them to a different location.

If your toddler is being rough with objects, you can simply remove the object calmly and without awarding the child any attention.

Step 3 - Give the Attention to the Wounded First

Step 3 is crucial in determining the frequency and intensity of these fights. Give your attention to the wounded first. We're sending the following messages:

-   Teaches the aggressor that he won't be getting any attention for this behavior.

- Teaches the aggressor that he is not the priority when someone is hurt.
- Reduces your chances of a power struggle, which might increase the undesired behavior.
- Helps you keep your cool through this process since you're not confronting the person who might anger you more.
- Teaches your child that his aggressive actions have negative consequences on someone (you're teaching him to relate and have more empathy).

Step 4 - Encourage your Kid to Make Amends

"Oh Sarah, look at poor Patty, she's hurt. She's holding her head where she got hit. What can we do to make her feel better?" Odds are, your child will just stare at you the first few times. So, just keep going. "Come here Patty, let's get you some ice. Sarah, I want you to grab the ice pack from the freezer and bring it over." Teach your toddler how to make amends. "Sarah, why don't you grab one of your toys that would make Patty feel better." When you bring kids in to repair their actions, you show them that you have faith in them and that you don't just see them as troublemakers or aggressors. You're not putting labels on them, which allows them to have the courage to shape their own identity. Another key takeaway from this step is that you are teaching your child to rise above and be the first to reach out and make amends regardless of the reason for the aggression.

This change won't happen overnight - you must model this process a few times before you see change. And in my experience, girls will catch on much faster than boys.

Step 5 - Take Some Space

Use step 5 as needed, depending on the severity of the situation and your child's temperament.

When allowed to be alone in a calming environment, some kids defuse their emotions faster. It's not a kind of punishment but a useful technique for teaching kids how to calm down and get themselves under control again. Keep in mind your child's age, stage of growth, and personality.

"I see a very angry little boy; come on, Jack, let's go upstairs and do a calm-down activity before we play with Sally again."

Step 6 - Relate & Offer Alternatives

Step 6 does not need to happen right away. In fact, don't move into step 6 until you feel like you and the toddler are both in the right mental state. Depending on your child's age, you might adjust what you say.

The formula is as follows:

1. Inquire after the reason for the aggression.
2. Relate to the emotion behind the anger and validate it.
3. Disaffirm the aggressive behavior.
4. Offer alternative options / Ask the child to offer alternative options.

"Honey, let's talk about what happened earlier. Can you tell me why you got angry?" If you don't get an answer, look around for clues: "I see that your legos got messed up. Is that what made you angry?" Follow up with, "I can understand how frustrating it must be when your brother destroys your legos. The problem is hitting is not allowed. What else can you do when you're angry?" Or "Next time, call for help. Say, 'Mom, take Evan away.'"

This technique worked beautifully when my twins were 18 months old, and their four-month-old sister would crawl up to them and mess their toys up. They used to shove her away. I had to teach them to say, "Mom, take Lily away." I made them repeat it back to me a few times to give them the confidence that they can say it. I also hovered and waited until an incident was about to happen and instructed them to say it. They caught on pretty quickly for their young age.

Make it clear to your kid that you understand what he wants to do: "I can see that you want to build a tower with those blocks. The problem is throwing them across the room isn't the right way to express your excitement. Let's find a safer way to enjoy building together." Or, "I notice that you're feeling disappointed because your friend got a turn on the swing first. It was nice of you to let him go first. It's important to take turns and share. Should we go to the slide while we wait for your turn?"

Teach your kid the appropriate behaviors to reach his goals or channel his enthusiasm. Your kid is more likely to repeat the undesirable behavior if you interrupt them without providing a suitable replacement.

If your toddler enjoys playing with water and dumping their sippy cup, consider taking her outdoors or into the bathtub.

If she enjoys throwing things, make a game out of tossing soft balls into a basket or box.

Step 7 - Logical Consequence

Step 7 is optional. You will have to use your judgment on when to use it. In my house, step 7 happens on the second offense of the same nature - second time hitting or second time biting- or when the aggression is directed at an object.

If your youngster ruins their own belongings, a logical consequence may also be the best option. Don't purchase a new toy if your toddler deliberately tosses and destroys it. It's an important lesson to teach. Sometimes, we simply don't get second chances. Better to learn that when the stakes are low.

Another logical consequence is to remove items when they are being misused or rough handled. For example, if Anthony is taking out his aggression on train tracks, then the train tracks get put away for a week. If Izzy dumps potties full of pee when she's enraged, then the potties are removed from the house, and she can get herself up on a toilet until she shows signs or vocalizes that she is done with that behavior.

However, certain things can't be moved easily, like a couch or chair. In that case, we establish a logical consequence.

Logical consequences need to follow the Five R rule:

- Respectful. No blaming, shaming, or inflicting pain.
- Related. Connected to the bad behavior. Otherwise, it feels like an unfair punishment - resentment will follow, and the lesson will be lost.
- Reasonable in duration. "For a year or a month" might be too long for a toddler.
- Revealed ahead of time so that the child can make an informed decision.
- Repeated back so that we are sure that the child understands and retains the consequence.

Jamie and Jenny are having a hard time playing on the swings together. "Girls, we have a new rule. If you can't play on the swings without hitting, then we can't come to the playground for a couple of days. Now, repeat this rule back to me so that I can make sure that we all know it."

You'll find that sometimes when the child vocalizes the rule, the unwanted behavior stops. They acknowledge that there is now a consequence and that hitting is not worth it anymore.

WHY NOT PUNISHMENTS, TIMEOUTS, OR REWARDS?

Punishments, timeouts as punishment, and rewards all hinder the educative process of managing big emotions in a healthy way. They focus too much on external factors and take the focus away from internal ones. Our goal is to teach our toddlers what to do when they have those big emotions, not make them too scared to express them or force their compliance with treats and rewards. That is manipulation. When external factors are utilized to obtain compliance, we're not really teaching children anything. We're just delaying the lesson until those external factors can no longer influence our children.

I want my children to play nicely and communicate well when they are upset because they know how to do it and not because they are scared that they will get a timeout or be punished if they don't.

Another point I'd like to bring up is the sustainability of punishments. You might be able to implement punishments on toddlers and little kids, but once your children are teenagers, forcing them into a timeout might be a bit trickier. You'll end up with kids that sneak behind your back and hide things from you to avoid punishments.

I simply don't like external factors, whether negative or positive. Just like how I don't want my children to do the right thing simply out of fear, I also don't want them to do the right thing because they might get a reward in exchange. That's not how life works. Good behavior is not a quid pro quo.

The other issue I see with rewards or good behavior charts is that it can cause sibling jealousy and label your child's "goodness" based on a piece of paper or how many treats they got that day. Not to mention, it's another thing for me to keep track of and manage. I'd rather focus my time and energy on being present with my children, reading books, and playing with them.

I'd like to be completely transparent here. I've seen families use rewards and punishments to achieve compliance, and it has worked for them while their kids were young.

I have also tried it myself. It did not work for me. My children are too strong-willed. Punishments and timeouts resulted in an increased frequency of the offense, left me with a lot of anger and frustration, and, quite honestly, caused some damage to my relationship, specifically with my oldest daughter. Izzy is highly sensitive and takes chastisement very personally. She also does not forget a thing. I could feel her anger and resentment. She withdrew into herself, became more aggressive, and started lashing out at us and her siblings. It was a huge contributor to what started my positive parenting journey.

LONG-TERM SOLUTIONS FOR PREVENTING AGGRESSION

Step 1: Observe and Learn

The answers to the following questions may shed light on the underlying causes of your child's behavior. With this knowledge, you can formulate an appropriate long-term response.

What is currently happening in your child's world? Where does this behavior occur? Is it limited to specific environments such as home, childcare, the shopping center, or Grandma's house? Or does it happen across multiple environments your child frequents?

Is the behavior confined to one place, or could it be triggered by the environment itself, such as an overly busy, bright, or overwhelming setting?

Are you or a small number of individuals the target of this behavior? Or does the kid sometimes act out toward others who are not directly involved in their life?

At what times does this behavior typically occur? For instance, does it happen when your child is tired and nearing naptime or during transitions from one activity to another? These types of pressures often act as catalysts for challenging behavior.

When did your kid start acting out like this? Did you say something like, "It's time to stop playing and get in the car." Had another kid just yanked a toy from his grasp?

Is your kid uncomfortable, anxious, or sad because of something that has happened recently? Does he feel less protected and secure? Your kid may have less self-control after experiencing life changes such as a childcare change, a relocation, the birth or death of a family member, or the adoption of a new pet.

Other crucial things to take into account:

Developmental Stage.

Is your toddler's behavior consistent with what you would expect from a kid of this age? Biting once a week is probably not cause for alarm, but biting many times a week might be.

Child's Temperament.

Is there a chance your child's temperament plays a role in their actions? For instance, during free play at a daycare, a very passionate and sensitive toddler may experience sensory overload. He may resort to biting; maybe he wants to keep others at bay for his own safety. When left with a new babysitter, a toddler who takes time to warm up to others may strike a parent. Anger is a common way young children (and many adults) show fear.

Your own personality and life experiences.

Do you find this behavior especially challenging? And if so, why? Sometimes, a parent's response to their child's behavior is influenced by their upbringing. For instance, if a parent had strict rules about how to behave in a restaurant while growing up, they might react similarly when their own child misbehaves in a dining setting. They might become easily frustrated or lose their patience. Understanding these relationships enables you to respond to your child's behavior in ways that are appropriate for her age, developmental stage, and personality type.

What's your situation?

How do you manage your emotions when your kid exhibits violent behavior? Can you control your reaction till you've calmed down? How well do you think you are assisting your kid in managing his aggressive feelings? What strategies have proven effective? What approaches have not been successful? Can you identify the reasons behind their effectiveness or lack thereof? What, in your opinion, is your kid learning from the way you handle their violent behavior?

Am I meeting my kid's needs?

Perhaps the most important question of all. If your child's needs aren't being met, then they will find negative ways for you to meet them. Go back to Chapter 1, work through the chapters, and implement changes.

Step 2: React to what your kid is
trying to say or do, not what he is doing.

Consider prevention.

Make use of your knowledge about your kid to prepare ahead of time. If you know he is nervous around new people, spend time looking through the family photo album in the weeks leading up to a big family gathering so he becomes familiar with extended family members. You can even create a pretend picnic scenario during playtime with her Aunt Emily and Uncle Mark to help her get more comfortable. Bring your kid's favorite books and stuffed animals to keep her company.

When you arrive at the event, encourage your loved ones to wait until your child has warmed up to his new environment before giving him a big hug. It will help them bond with your kid to wait until she's ready.

By using these tactics, you are not "caving in" to your kid but rather assisting him in managing a really challenging situation. This prepares her to meet new people in unfamiliar environments, such as a new school.

<u>Give notice of impending changes in advance.</u>

"We have one more book to read before it's time to drive home. What book would you most want to read?" Giving children options might make them feel more in control and less aggressive.

Help your child figure out how he feels and what he is doing. Help him learn how to deal with his feelings in a healthy way. For example, you might tell your child who has trouble switching between tasks, "I know it's hard for you to stop playing so you can get in the car and go to nanas. Why don't you bring along your favorite book to read? Or maybe we can play "I Spy" on our way. What would you rather do?"

Over time, this teaches your youngster coping mechanisms to deal with difficult situations. Tell younger children how they are feeling, and then change the subject. "You're upset that your dad turned off the TV. Take a look at this nice ball and the way it bounces." Again, don't use "but" after acknowledging feelings.

Constructive Time-out.

When properly implemented, time-outs teach kids to step back when their emotions are high and take care of themselves instead of engaging in unhealthy encounters. Ideally, time-out is for children to use on themselves before acting violently. The purpose of this time-out is not to penalize the child but to provide them with an opportunity to use calming techniques before returning to regular activities. At first, you will almost certainly need to be there with your child to guide them through these exercises.

Calm Down techniques.

Teach your child calm-down techniques for when they feel out of control. Consider deep belly breathing, counting, coloring, and reading. You'll have to practice these with them when everyone is calm and happy. Use the same trigger words at the beginning of each exercise so your child is more likely to recognize them during an episode. "Let's do our deep breathing" or "Let's go to a quiet room".

Step 3: Teach your kid, who is starting
to grasp reasoning and logical thought,
to draw conclusions from their own activities.

Show your child what happened after he did something wrong. For example, "Emily started to cry after you hit her. It was painful. She was sad and angry. She no longer wanted to play with you, which made you sad." Think about better decisions your kid could make in the future. "What other options do you have besides hitting if Emily steals your doll?" If your kid is at a loss for words (which is perfectly normal), you may propose some tactics, like encouraging her to say, "That is my doll. Please return it," "I wasn't done playing with that," before presenting Emily with a different doll. Reassure your kid that you are there for her whenever she needs you. If you give them some suggestions, they may be able to come up with further ideas on their own. Learning to replace undesirable behavior with more desirable alternatives is an important aspect of maturing self-control. It is also an important skill to have in school and life in general.

CHAPTER 8

Siblings

The Fuss Between The Best of Friends

Bullying between siblings is real and can lead to both mental and physical illness. A 2013 study on children found that kids with violent siblings are more likely to have mental health problems. Also, imagine the stress that accompanies bullying, stress that you can't get away from, and how much it would interfere with a child's learning abilities and social and emotional development.

One of my fears is that my children might grow up to not be friends, or worse, on unfriendly terms. Nobody wants their kids to fight. And, when the fighting is too frequent, it can be annoying, frustrating, make you want to scream, and pull your hair out. "Just get along!" or "Quit it!" are great to scream some of that frustration out of you, but they don't achieve much.

Here's the thing: fighting is inevitable. It comes hand in hand with free will and different personalities. The best thing we can do for our children is not eliminate fights but teach them healthy ways to fight and resolve them. We want them to master that invaluable skill. It will help them well into adulthood.

THE PEACEFUL HOME

Creating a peaceful home is a crucial part of child development. We want our kids to feel as safe as can be at home so that their learning process is not disrupted.

Stop violence - no matter how small.

Have a code that says they can't hit, kick, spit, bite, give wedgies, push pencils into the skin, or do anything violent.

Make respect an unbreakable principle.

There should be no emotional violence of any kind. Teasing, bullying, shaming, and saying hurtful things are all ways of inflicting pain on others. Teach your children to see things from other people's perspectives and treat them with the same dignity and respect they would like for themselves.

The foundation and strategies taught through this book and this chapter will help reinforce those two points without drawing too much attention to them and unwittingly giving your kids ideas on how to push your buttons.

So how do we make best friends out of our children?

STRATEGIES FOR FOSTERING POSITIVE SIBLING RELATIONSHIPS

When nurturing healthy sibling relationships, we all strive to create an environment of love and harmony. However, we understand that conflicts between siblings can sometimes arise unexpectedly, catching parents off guard or occurring when they are not present to intervene. Here are some ideas on how to prevent disagreements in the first place.

Make sure each child gets enough one-on-one time.

One-on-one time does wonders for your child's sense of security, belonging, and significance. This will allow each child to "shine" to you, the most important person to them, thus reducing jealousy.

Encourage one-on-one time between siblings.

We've already established how important one-on-one time is to fortify the bond between parent and child. So why not encourage children to do one-on-one with each other? Give them 10 minutes to do one-on-one together. You can ask your older child to take charge. And pick a couple of activities for their younger sibling to choose from. It will do wonders for their relationship.

Stopping new baby jealousy.

A common issue, especially for toddlers, is the arrival of a new baby. Typically, a new baby makes them feel usurped and sets the dynamic for the rest of the relationship. A few tweaks of your wording can easily remedy that. Whenever you're talking about the baby, refer to them as "your brother," "your sister," "Stella's baby brother," or "Stella's baby sister." Bring them in on the responsibility and ownership.

Ask them to help change diapers or pick out outfits for their baby. Ask them to read a book for the baby or show them how the baby suckles. If they get jealous of the nursing, then let them try (talking toddlers here). Odds are they'll give it a go and lose interest in a second. If you have a young toddler who could still be nursing and take it up again(it's very unlikely), then great! It's so healthy for them and it'll help you lose the baby weight faster since nursing takes up so many calories.

Use baby talk to your advantage. Instead of cooing, "Oh, who's a good baby? You're so cute," when looking at your newest bundle of joy, say in your best cooing voice, "Oh, did you know what your big brother did today? He kicked the ball, and it went so high! I bet you can't wait to play with your big brother!"

Stay on top of one-on-one time with your other kids if you can manage it. If not, try to give them some extra love before bedtime. Explain to them that you are recovering and need a few days to get back on your feet and that you love them very much.

Comparing kids.

Don't compare your children to each other, especially not in front of each other. Kids are always trying to impress us with their unique personalities and, more importantly, win our approval. When we compare ourselves to others, we are pointing out that something about ourselves is not good enough.

If siblings feel lacking when compared to each other, they will fight even more.

"Freya is more adventurous than Maya" will make Maya resent her sister for being seen as more than her.

No Labels.

Labels are also a form of comparison. "Claire is the pretty one." Claire's sister might then think she is not pretty. Claire might believe that pretty is all she'll ever be or all that is expected of her. "Alex is the athletic one," "Jenny is the outgoing one."

Beware of well-intentioned labeling, too. I've done this countless times when I leave my kids with a sitter. "Ask Izzy if you need any help." Yes, Izzy is very attentive and helpful. Still, by singling her out to a person of authority, a.k.a. sitter or teacher, I'm making them biased and, therefore, more likely to view her and treat her differently and less likely to give everyone else an equal opportunity. The truth is, Anthony is just as attentive but maybe not as responsive and could use the practice much more than Izzy. Negative labeling is also a huge nuisance: "Brandon is the naughty one," "Jake is the unattentive one." Comments like, "Anthony can be a bit naughty," might make the teacher expect him to lash out and treat him more sternly - whether intentional or not.

Plan organized family time.

Once a week, even if it's just for an hour, plan something for the whole family to do together, like a special meal, exercise, outing, or game. Focus on games that foster team building rather than competitiveness. Build a family spirit and kinship. By modeling appropriate social behavior and emphasizing the value of turn-taking, you help your children develop a strong sense of self-worth, civility, and love.

Don't create unnecessary competition.

Yes, the world is full of competition. The kids will likely be confronted with that fact very quickly. So why make your home competitive, too? Why not make it a safe haven instead? I prefer my children to be on the same team rather than against each other. We unconsciously pit our kids against each other. Comments like, "Let's see who can climb up the stairs the fastest," or "Who can eat the quickest," to spur kids into action can be easily replaced with, "If we beat the timer to get dressed, then we can read an extra book before bed," or "When everyone's food is eaten then we can go to the park."

There is no need for them to view each other as adversaries.

Of course, using these tactics doesn't imply that children won't ever fight; disagreements are part of human nature. So, what can we do to help children deal with conflict?

Model Healthy Conflict Resolution.

It's easier to get through life when we know how to express ourselves and listen to others respectfully. The best way to teach our children how to do that is by modeling healthy conflict resolution. We parents tend to keep our fighting private and away from our kids. The problem with that is that we're robbing our children of chances of learning how to resolve conflict. After all, kids learn the most from watching their parents.

Now, I'm not saying have all your fights in front of your kids; some things really ought to be private, but allow room for some disagreements to be in front of them.

Discuss this with your partner, especially if you have a hard time resolving conflicts respectfully, and make sure that you're both on the same page:

- Listening attentively
- Apologizing for your part
- Compromising

You are the best example for your kids to follow. They will learn to talk things out peacefully and civilly if they witness you doing the same. They need to see you apologize if you want them to be able to apologize to others. Seeing adults with different viewpoints engage in civil discourse will teach them to do the same. They will accept that others may have different opinions than their own.

If you're a single parent, don't worry. You can do these with a friend or grandparent and even with your kid, as I'm sure you will have conflict with them.

You are the problem-solving mentor for your kids. They learn from you how to negotiate, control their anger, and be fair players. It's far better than being a judge who breaks up fights or steps in when they start to get out of hand and might be seen as harboring favorites.

Give the Right Kind of Attention.

Instead of giving attention to negative behavior, which would most likely result in more negative behavior, try giving attention to the positive behaviors.

"Izzy, hurry up and buckle in your car seat" can be replaced with, "Oh, Anthony, you're all buckled up. I hear a click from Lily's car seat. Oh look, Jamie's all buckled up, too." Izzy will hurry up and get buckled just to get recognized, "I heard a click from Izzy's car seat! Let me know when you're all buckled up and ready to go."

Some other examples:

"Jenny is bringing her plate to the sink - thank you, Jenny!"

"Arthur is washing his hands - look how clean you are!"

"Kelly is setting the tables - you got all the plates already!"

Focus on the ones that are doing well rather than the troublemakers. After all, they are the ones who deserve attention and recognition.

When your kids are acting nicely, point it out and show them that you noticed it. Children are more likely to repeat a behavior when you praise them for it clearly and explicitly. Here are some examples:

"I love how you're both taking turns on the trampoline."

"You guys are all playing and sharing so well."

"Hey, you guys did a great job problem-solving. You must be very proud of yourselves."

A great way to give recognition without being too obvious is to allow your children to "eavesdrop" on a conversation. Hop on a pretend phone call with your spouse or parent. Tell them how

Trevor helped you clean up the whole kitchen after breakfast; and make sure Trevor is within earshot.

HANDLING FIGHTS CONSTRUCTIVELY

When parents get involved, we tend to take sides, which often makes the situation worse. We put kids in a box and tell them, "Come on, you're older," " She's a little girl, and you're a big boy," or "You've had that doll for a while; just share with her," etc.

Sometimes, without fully understanding the circumstances, we intervene and impose strict consequences. But what if we take a different approach and encourage our children to listen to one another, grow in emotional intelligence, and seek out opportunities for compromise and conflict resolution?

Yesterday, my daughters got into it again. Three-and-a-half-year-old Izzy was playing with a doll that two-year-old Lily wanted. This sparked a lively chase in our living room. It wasn't a playful chase since Lily was sobbing and screaming while running after her older sister.

Izzy got away, not by being mean or getting angry, but by ignoring her sister and expertly eluding her grip. So, I had no grounds to interfere without seeming like I was taking sides, but I knew a fight was about to erupt.

So, I stood in the background and described what I thought was happening. "I can see that you both want the doll. I also see that you're both feeling a bit upset."

There were times when I questioned my strategy and wondered whether I should step in to halt the fighting. But then Lily stopped trying to grab the doll and just stood beside her sister. Even though she was still crying, it wasn't as bad.

"It looks like she just wants to stand next to you now, Izzy." I couldn't help but say.

Izzy ran across the room, and Lily followed her. I could tell they were happier now. They played side by side for a few minutes, and then Izzy handed her little sister the doll and said, "I'm all done playing with it now. You can have it." "Thank you," said Lily with a big smile.

Here are a few encouraging lessons my kids picked up from this event. What my oldest daughter picked up was:

"My parents understand that I don't always have to give in to my sister just because she's younger. They know that my feelings and wants are just as important as hers. They don't pick sides or think I'm being mean when I want to be in charge. They make sure I don't hurt my sister, but they don't criticize me for wanting to be in control. They don't make me give up my turn."

These teachings strengthen the bond between us as parents and our children and provide them with a solid feeling of emotional safety and stability. If, on the other hand, we mistreat our bigger kids or judge them, which can be hard not to do, we create a rift between us and the child and between siblings. Fear takes over, which often leads to more mean or violent behavior. Children, like adults, act out more severely when they feel bad.

My younger daughter, on the other hand, picked up:

"I know how to stand up for myself with my sister. I don't need my mom and dad to save me. When I don't get what I want, it makes me feel bad at the time, and I can talk about it, but eventually, I get over it."

Both children picked up:

"Our parents believe in us and trust that we can handle struggles and find solutions." A priceless affirmation, considering that life is full of problems.

Children learn best by doing. Offering children a secure - physical and emotional - space to experience the highs and lows of relationships with their siblings and peers is the best way to teach them to cope. Conflicts like this offer invaluable chances to develop problem-solving, self-assurance, emotional resilience, social intelligence, and the ability to establish and maintain trusting relationships.

Some key takeaways when stepping in:

Remain calm

Keep your cool, even if you're boiling with rage. Exhale and talk without agitation. In most cases, this works considerably better than yelling.

Remain unbiased

Don't choose a side based on the ages of your children. Do not automatically side with the victim. There may be a backstory that you are not privy to. You also don't want to set the precedent that being a victim will get you sympathy and attention.

Describe what you see

"I see two little girls that want to play with the same doll."
"I see a little girl whose puzzle is being stepped on."
"I see a baby who wants his toys back."
Describing what is happening might help the children reexamine the situation and fix their behavior.

Prompt some problem-solving

If describing the situation doesn't cut it, then try problem-solving. "We have a problem; I see two little girls that want the same doll. What can we do about this problem?"

If your children are fighting over an item, removing it whilst discussing the solution is best. "I'm going to put the dolly up high until we figure out the solution to our problem."

"What can we do about this?" You might have to offer additional suggestions if your children are very young. "Should we take five-minute turns or play together?" Make sure both parties agree to the solution before bringing the doll back. If they can't, it's too bad. No doll.

Separate them

Move the kids away from each other, but not necessarily to different rooms. Just put some space between them and, again, stay neutral, even if one of the kids is much younger. Take the younger sibling's hand and say, "Let's go sit on the couch together and take some time to calm down." At the same time, ask the older sibling to sit and take a break.

Is it really a fight, or are they looking for some attention?

Kids like to fight in front of their parents sometimes. They may be seeking your implicit approval, want to demonstrate their superior physical prowess, or just want some attention. You shouldn't get involved if it seems like harmless play fighting rather than anything more serious. Just be there for them and let them know you know they can work things out without you. After a while, you can leave the room knowing that the fighting will stop since there's no one there to watch.

Play fighting

Play fighting is very fun, especially for boys. As long as they are messing around and having fun and no one is in danger, you should leave them alone. Play fighting, however, can very quickly turn into real fighting. And sometimes, the word "stop" can be playful, just as it can be serious. Kids might have difficulty discerning between the tone of voice and figuring out if the other person is really asking them to stop. If this is an issue in your house, consider picking a safe word instead of "stop," like "potato." Teach your kids that the roughhousing must end once the word "potato" is said. Role-playing this scenario is the best way to teach them.

Teach conflict resolution

Here's how we can help our children work through conflict resolution.

1. Make sure that everyone is calm enough to talk.
2. Each story will have two sides. Listen to each kid without passing judgment or interrupting. Children usually feel better after talking to their parents about their problems, particularly if they know they will be heard without bias. Encourage your children to use the "I feel..." statement instead of attacking the other person. "I feel really angry when my Lego tower is knocked down," instead of "Kelly is so mean; she's always destroying my tower." It will help your children relate, not get defensive, and not take on labels such as bully, victim, etc..
3. Ask each child to repeat their siblings' perspective. This step is so helpful for practicing empathy.
4. Ask everyone to apologize for their wrongdoing.
5. Look for solutions and what to do next time.
6. Make sure that everyone leaves the table satisfied with the outcome.

It is imperative to note that your only role through this process is to facilitate communication. You are not offering commentary or siding with any one of your children. You'll cause more harm than good. Teaching our kids to share and be nice to one another won't happen if we take sides and tell them what to do during an argument.

Make peace among siblings a family goal.

Tell your kids that your family is a team. A harmonious and loving family unit requires teamwork from everyone involved, including mom, dad, and the kids. When family members fight, it hurts the whole team. Celebrate each other's successes and share each other's struggles and burdens. Start small with a supportive conversation and move into action. "How was your day, honey?" "Do you need me to help with anything?" "Daddy finished a very big project at work today, so we're gonna celebrate and make a cake." "Your sister is struggling with putting her new shoes on. I'd like you to show her how to please." "I need help bringing all the groceries in from the car." Don't forget to celebrate the wins together, too. "Lily knows all her letters now! Yay! Your little sister is growing so fast! Should we sing the ABC song together with her?"

Encourage children to speak up for themselves.

Tell your child to stop blaming their feelings on their sibling and instead look within. For instance, if your kid feels that their sibling is unfairly choosing the games they will play all the time, they should express their feelings rather than attack the other person. "I'd like to pick the game this time." "I feel annoyed that I haven't gotten to pick a game this week." "Can I have a turn, please?" Even an 18-month-old can be taught to stick their hand out and say, "Turn please," instead of hitting or screaming.

PARENTING JOURNEY

It was getting to the end of a particularly challenging day. I was watching Anthony wiggle around while holding his crotch. "Honey, you need to go potty. Go find the bathroom." Anthony, "I'm not dancing," as he does the peepee dance. After several unsuccessful attempts to get him to the bathroom, I gave up. Fifteen minutes later, he bolted to the bathroom. Unfortunately, in his haste, some of the pee went on his shorts. "My pants and undies are wet!" he cried. I sighed, "Alright, take them off; let's put them in the laundry basket and get you some new ones." As we start walking up the stairs, Anthony makes the most grotesque spit bubbles and lets them loose all over my carpeted stairs. I snapped. His bare bottom was right there, and I couldn't help but give his tush a little smack. "Hey! Stop that!"

Dang it! I shouldn't have done that! I immediately thought to myself, regretting the impulse. Anthony proceeded to scream in rage. He whirled around, pointed a finger at me, and shouted, "I'm disappointed in you!"

I was beyond shocked. Talk about a humbling moment. I messed up and didn't express my frustration the right way, but my three-and-a-half-year-old was able to use his words when angry.

You can arm yourself with all the right knowledge and tools, but if you, the parent, are overwhelmed, it is so easy to take a wrong turn and revert to being a reactive parent rather than a proactive one.

I don't want to leave you with dread that you always have to be in control and can't ever let some rage out. So, I'll let you in on a secret. You can scream your frustration just as you would expect your child to. If you're desperate, feel free to yell, "I'm getting angry!!!" or "I'm getting frustrated!" Scream your emotions out if you must. It's okay for your children to understand that you have limits, too. Focus on what you're feeling and let it out. Be careful not to direct your screaming at them.

Parenting is a journey; like any journey, it has its fair share of twists, turns, and setbacks. Don't let them discourage you, but power through them. Keep your end goal in sight, and look for those glimpses of encouragement.

The three steps in each area discussed in this book are the same.

1. Understand the behavior
2. Deal with the behavior with understanding and patience
3. Proactively prevent it from repeating itself

Every day brings new chances to grow and learn for our kids and us. With the information and ideas in this book, you have the power to help your child grow in security and love.

Be patient and gentle with yourself and your child as you take the time to put the methods and approaches into practice.

Remember, challenges come hand in hand with parenting. No matter how well we plan, things can still go wrong. Your toddler, who used to sleep well, now wakes up four or five times a night. A good eater is now turning down his favorite foods! Things happen; it's par for the course.

This book will serve as a resource you can keep coming back to when you face new issues as a parent.

I hope that it brings you some solace to remember that there is no such thing as flawless parenting, ideal kids, or perfect parents. Every one of us is doing our best with the information we have, and perhaps as we learn more, we'll be able to do more.

If you enjoyed this book and found it helpful, please leave a review on your favorite bookselling platform. They really do help. I hope that even amid challenges, you remember to laugh, smile, and enjoy each moment.

As older moms always tell me, you'll miss them being so little when they're all grown up.

RESOURCES

5 strategies that prevent most misbehavior.
(n.d.). https://www.ahaparenting.com/
read/3-Strategies-That-Prevent-Most-Misbehavior

8 Ways to Build (and Keep) Trust with Your Kids.
(n.d.). Yummy Mummy Club | yummymummyclub.
ca. https://www.yummymummyclub.ca/blogs/
andrea-nair-connect-four-parenting/20141203/
the-eight-actions-parents-can-do-to-increase-trust

Active listening | Communicating | Essentials |
Parenting Information | CDC. (n.d.-a). https://www.
cdc.gov/parents/essentials/toddlersandpreschoolers/
communication/activelistening.html

Active listening | Communicating | Essentials |
Parenting Information | CDC. (n.d.-b). https://www.
cdc.gov/parents/essentials/toddlersandpreschoolers/
communication/activelistening.html

Admin. (2019a, August 19). Sibling Rivalry - How much
is too much? - Parenting NI. Parenting NI. https://www.
parentingni.org/blog/sibling-rivalry-how-much-is-too-much/

Admin. (2019b, August 19). Sibling Rivalry - How much
is too much? - Parenting NI. Parenting NI. https://www.
parentingni.org/blog/sibling-rivalry-how-much-is-too-much/

Albertsen, M. (2022). Sibling Rivalry: My kids are arguing all the time, what can I do? KiddyCharts. https://www.kiddycharts.com/discipline/ sibling-rivalry-my-kids-are-arguing-all-the-time-what-can-i-do/

Alexander, F., & Alexander, F. (2023). How to Prioritize Yourself First As A Mom Without Feeling Guilty. Mama & Money. https://mamaandmoney.com/prioritize-yourself/

Alexander, L. (2023). How to Stop a Whining Child (Pro Tips from a Pediatrician). Mom Loves Best. https://momlovesbest.com/stop-whining-child

Amazon.com: How to Talk So Kids Will Listen & Listen So Kids Will Talk (The How To Talk Series) eBook : Faber, Adele, Mazlish, Elaine: Kindle Store. (n.d.). https://www.amazon.com/ How-Talk-Kids-Will-Listen-ebook/dp/B005GG0MXI/ref=tmm_ kin_swatch_0?_encoding=UTF8&qid=1695346669&sr=8-1

Auger, S. (n.d.). The Importance of Spending One-on-One Time with Your Children. https://www.safesplash.com/blog/the-importance-of-spending-one-on-one-time-with-your-children

auroradesignstudio. (n.d.). Home. The Childrens Project. https://emotionallyhealthychildren.org/

Autuori-Dedic, J. (2023). 4 Big emotions to talk about with little kids. Parents. https://www.parents. com/toddlers-preschoolers/development/intellectual/ list-of-emotions-to-talk-about-with-kids/

Becky. (2023). How to raise emotionally healthy kids. Emotionally Healthy Kids. https://emotionallyhealthykids. com/how-to-raise-emotionally-healthy-kids/

Begin Learning Team. (2023, June 7). How To Cope With Kids Fighting: Tips For Parents - Begin Learning. Begin Learning. https://www.learnwithhomer. com/homer-blog/6939/kids-fighting/

Bennett, E. (2022, June 15). What are the Emotional Needs of a Child? The Hub | High Speed Training. https://www. highspeedtraining.co.uk/hub/emotional-needs-of-a-child/

Bhattacharjee, A. (2022, January 4). 14 Self-care Tips for Mom-sanity - Why is it necessary for mothers to do self-care? - Democratic Naari. Democratic Naari. https:// democraticnaari.com/2022/01/04/14-self-care-tips-for-mom-sanity-why-is-it-necessary-for-mothers-to-do-self-care/

Bigley II, J. (2023, March 8). 10 tips for dealing with sibling Rivalry. Cleveland Clinic. https:// health.clevelandclinic.org/sibling-rivalry/

Bly, J. (2018). How to Build a Trusting Relationship with Your Child. The Deliberate Mom. https://thedeliberatemom. com/trusting-relationship-with-your-child/

Buch, M. (2022a). Why Self-Care Is Critical For A Parent's Well-Being. Time To Get Some Me Time. Shri Harini Media Ltd. https://www.parentcircle. com/importance-of-self-care-for-parents/article

Buch, M. (2022b). Why Self-Care Is Critical For A Parent's Well-Being. Time To Get Some Me Time. Shri Harini Media Ltd. https://www.parentcircle. com/importance-of-self-care-for-parents/article

Candidate, B. S. M. P. (2023). Positive Reinforcement for kids: 11+ examples for parents. PositivePsychology.com. https://positivepsychology.com/parenting-positive-reinforcement/

Childcare. (2019, August 15). Establishing predictable routines in a child care setting – eXtension Alliance for Better Child Care. https://childcare.extension.org/establishing-predictable-routines-in-a-child-care-setting/

CNP, K. B. A. (2021). Self-care tips for moms. Mayo Clinic Health System. https://www.mayoclinichealthsystem.org/hometown-health/speaking-of-health/self-care-tips-for-moms

Collective, A. L. T. (2022). 5 Situations Leading to Sibling Fights and How To Handle Them. Anchor Light Therapy Collective. https://anchorlighttherapy.com/5-situations-leading-to-sibling-fights-and-how-to-handle-them/

Common challenges for parents of toddlers and young children. (n.d.). https://myfirstapp.com/blog/common-challenges-for-parents-of-toddlers-and-young-children/

Coping with Sibling Rivalry. (2018, October 26). The Center for Parenting Education. https://centerforparentingeducation.org/library-of-articles/sibling-rivalry/coping-sibling-rivalry/

Currie, J. (2020). 11 Sure-Fire ways to stop sibling fighting and to encourage kids to get along. Happy Hooligans. https://happyhooligans.ca/ways-to-stop-sibling-fighting/

Dreisbach, S., Dunn, J., & O'Connor, G. (2023, June 29). How to deal with toddler temper tantrums. Parents. https://www.parents.com/toddlers-preschoolers/discipline/tantrum/a-parents-guide-to-temper-tantrums/

Dubin, A. (2022). Power Struggles With Kids, Explained. Moshi. https://www.moshikids. com/articles/power-struggles-kids/

Educator, K. F. C. P. (2022). The Basic needs of a child: 9 Essential things every child needs to thrive. Self-Sufficient Kids. https://selfsufficientkids.com/basic-needs-of-a-child/

Emotions and play: preschoolers. (2021, March 22). Raising Children Network. https:// raisingchildren.net.au/preschoolers/play-learning/ play-preschooler-development/emotions-play-preschoolers

Field, J. (2020). Surviving the Holidays with Grace: 3 Strategies to Disarm Your Emotional Triggers. Prime Women | an Online Magazine. https://primewomen. com/wellness/strategies-to-disarm-emotional-triggers/

Five ways to help misbehaving kids. (n.d.). Greater Good. https://greatergood.berkeley.edu/article/ item/five_ways_to_help_misbehaving_kids

Garcia, N. (2023). 5 Ways to Stop a toddler power Struggle. Sleeping Should Be Easy. https:// sleepingshouldbeeasy.com/toddler-power-struggle/

Geddes, J. K., & Geddes, J. K. (2022). Losing your cool with your toddler. What to Expect. https://www. whattoexpect.com/toddler/ask-heidi/losing-your-cool.aspx

Godfrey, D. (2020a). Dealing with power struggles. Positive Parenting. https://www.positiveparenting. com/dealing-with-power-struggles/

Godfrey, D. (2020b). Dealing with power struggles. Positive Parenting. https://www.positiveparenting. com/dealing-with-power-struggles/

Godfrey, D. (2020c). Dealing with power struggles. Positive Parenting. https://www.positiveparenting. com/dealing-with-power-struggles/

Handling sibling fights. (2020, November 23). Raising Children Network. https://raisingchildren.net.au/ school-age/behaviour/friends-siblings/handling-fights

Hitching, G. (2022). Positive Reinforcement: What is It and How Does it Work? Science of People. https:// www.scienceofpeople.com/positive-reinforcement/

K, A. (2023, August 9). 5 Causes Of Aggression In Children & Tips To Deal With Them. MomJunction. https://www.momjunction.com/articles/ how-to-deal-with-an-aggressive-children-behavior_00712210/

Kallios, N. (2017). Children feel unheard by adults on key issues, UNICEF survey finds. SBS News. https:// www.sbs.com.au/news/article/children-feel-unheard-by-adults-on-key-issues-unicef-survey-finds/64h3yef6e

Karp, H. (2017). 'Magic Breathing' helps even the wildest kids calm down. Happiest Baby. https:// www.happiestbaby.com/blogs/toddler/calm-kids

Karp, H. (2020a). Toddler Discipline: 2 Tactics that really work. Happiest Baby. https://www. happiestbaby.com/blogs/toddler/toddler-discipline

Karp, H. (2020b). How to keep your cool when your toddler pushes your buttons. Happiest Baby. https://www.happiestbaby.com/blogs/toddler/keep-your-cool-with-toddler

Lcsw, A. M. (2020). Discipline Strategies to Manage Aggression in children. Verywell Family. https://www.verywellfamily.com/discipline-strategies-to-manage-aggression-in-children-1094953

Lcsw, A. M. (2021a). How to avoid power struggles with children. Verywell Family. https://www.verywellfamily.com/how-to-avoid-power-struggles-with-children-1094751

Lcsw, A. M. (2021b). 6 steps to put an end to whining. Verywell Family. https://www.verywellfamily.com/steps-to-getting-kids-to-stop-whining-1094950

Lcsw, A. M. (2021c). 6 steps to put an end to whining. Verywell Family. https://www.verywellfamily.com/steps-to-getting-kids-to-stop-whining-1094950

Lcsw, A. M. (2022). How to use positive reinforcement to improve behavior. Verywell Family. https://www.verywellfamily.com/positive-reinforcement-child-behavior-1094889

Lee, K. (2020). 8 Ways to Effectively Manage sibling fighting and rivalry. Verywell Family. https://www.verywellfamily.com/solutions-for-sibling-fighting-and-rivalry-620104

Marcin, A. (2021, September 24). Why toddlers need routine — and a sample schedule to get you started. Healthline. https://www.healthline.com/health/parenting/toddler-schedule

Martinelli, K., & PsyD, S. a. L. (2023). When Siblings Won't Stop Fighting. Child Mind Institute. https://childmind.org/article/when-siblings-wont-stop-fighting/

Martin-Gordon, R. (2022). Why Moms Should Take Care of Themselves First -- And Where to Start — CODDLE. CODDLE. https://www.coddle.co/blog3/2021/5/6/why/mom/should/take/care/of/themselves/and/where/to/start

Matthiessen, C. (2008, April 24). Why kids whine and how to stop them. WebMD. https://www.webmd.com/parenting/features/why-kids-whine-and-how-to-stop-them

McCarthy, C., MD. (2020). 6 reasons children need to play outside. Harvard Health. https://www.health.harvard.edu/blog/6-reasons-children-need-to-play-outside-2018052213880

McCready, A. (2023, June 26). When Sibling Fights turn Physical: Ultimate Guide to success. Positive Parenting Solutions. https://www.positiveparentingsolutions.com/parenting/sibling-fighting

Mcilroy, T. (2023a, August 23). The Emotional Needs of a Child: 24 Tips for Parents - Empowered Parents. Empowered Parents. https://empoweredparents.co/emotional-needs-of-a-child/

Mcilroy, T. (2023b, August 23). The Emotional Needs of a Child: 24 Tips for Parents - Empowered Parents. Empowered Parents. https://empoweredparents.co/emotional-needs-of-a-child/

McMahill, A. (2022a). Defiance and power struggles for your 2-Year-Old. ParentingMontana.org. https://parentingmontana.org/defiance-and-power-struggles-for-your-2-year-old/

McMahill, A. (2022b). Defiance and power struggles for your 2-Year-Old. ParentingMontana.org. https://parentingmontana.org/defiance-and-power-struggles-for-your-2-year-old/

McMahill, A. (2022c). Defiance and power struggles for your 2-Year-Old. ParentingMontana.org. https://parentingmontana. org/defiance-and-power-struggles-for-your-2-year-old/

Mistry, R., Stevens, G. D., Sareen, H., De Vogli, R., & Halfon, N. (2007). Parenting-Related stressors and Self-Reported Mental Health of Mothers with young children. American Journal of Public Health, 97(7), 1261–1268. https://doi.org/10.2105/ajph.2006.088161

Nair, A. (2021). 10 ways to defuse a power struggle - Today's Parent. Today's Parent. https://www.todaysparent. com/family/discipline/ways-to-defuse-a-power-struggle/

Nicoleschwarz. (2018). Taking control of your parenting triggers. Nicole Schwarz, LMFT. https:// imperfectfamilies.com/tantrums-scare-me/

None. (2022). When to Worry about Toddler Temper Tantrums. www.hopkinsallchildrens.org. https://www. hopkinsallchildrens.org/ACH-News/General-News/ When-to-Worry-about-Toddler-Temper-Tantrums

Parlakian, R. (2023, June 22). Aggressive Behavior in toddlers | ZERO TO THREE. ZERO TO THREE. https://www. zerotothree.org/resource/aggressive-behavior-in-toddlers/

Positive Parenting Learning Center Positive Parenting Solutions. (2009, March 1). Positive Parenting Solutions. https://www.positiveparentingsolutions.com/parenting-blog

Preventing aggression - Portico. (2016, February 11). https:// www.porticonetwork.ca/web/knowledgex-archive/educators/ elementary-grades/aggressive-behaviour/preventing-aggression

Preventing sibling fights: eight tips. (2020, November 23). Raising Children Network. https://raisingchildren.net.au/school-age/behaviour/friends-siblings/preventing-fights

Professional, C. C. M. (n.d.-a). Temper tantrums. Cleveland Clinic. https://my.clevelandclinic.org/health/articles/14406-temper-tantrums

Professional, C. C. M. (n.d.-b). Temper tantrums. Cleveland Clinic. https://my.clevelandclinic.org/health/articles/14406-temper-tantrums

Ricci, R. C., De Paulo, A. S. C., De Freitas, A. K. P. B., Ribeiro, I. C., Pires, L. S. A., Facina, M. E. L., Cabral, M. B., Parduci, N. V., Spegiorin, R. C., Bogado, S. S. G., Chociay, S., Carachesti, T. N., & Larroque, M. M. (2023, January 1). Impacts of technology on children's health: a systematic review. Revista Paulista De Pediatria. https://doi.org/10.1590/1984-0462/2023/41/2020504

Right, T. (2022, April 13). Social & Emotional Development In Early Childhood - Tickle Right. Tickle Right. https://tickleright.com/social-emotional-development-in-early-childhood/

Sears, B. (2020). 25 Ways to Talk So Kids Will Listen. Ask Dr Sears. https://www.askdrsears.com/topics/parenting/discipline-behavior/25-ways-talk-so-children-will-listen/

Sibonney, C. (2023). This might be why you're getting so mad at your kids - Today's Parent. Today's Parent. https://www.todaysparent.com/family/parenting/parenting-triggers/

Silva, R., MD, & Silva, R., MD. (2023a). What are some of the causes of aggression in children? Child Mind Institute. https://childmind.org/article/aggression-in-children-causes/

Silva, R., MD, & Silva, R., MD. (2023b). What are some of the causes of aggression in children? Child Mind Institute. https://childmind.org/article/aggression-in-children-causes/

Simperingham, G. (2022, June 2). Why do many parents struggle to cope with their child's cries? - Peaceful Parent Institute. Peaceful Parent Institute. https://www.peacefulparent.com/why-do-many-parents-struggle-to-cope-with-their-childs-cries/

Simperingham, G. (2023, June 2). Active listening improves communication in the parent child relationship. Peaceful Parent Institute. https://www.peacefulparent.com/active-listening-improves-the-parent-child-relationshi/

Singhal, M. (2021). Why Your Child Whines And How To Respond Effectively. Shri Harini Media Ltd. https://www.parentcircle.com/how-to-stop-kids-from-whining-and-complaining/article?gclid=CjwKCAjwxr2iBhBJEiwAdXECw5QVmow6sGsXeL9OPB8YqR8fxERa7AD5SswZJeUIphFj_Ns4YNliohoCwOQQAvD_BwE

Social and emotional development in early learning settings. (2023, September 21). https://www.ncsl.org/human-services/social-and-emotional-development-in-early-learning-settings

Staff, S. P. (2018). 13 Ways to Raise a caring and Compassionate Child. www.scholastic.com. https://www.scholastic.com/parents/family-life/social-emotional-learning/social-skills-for-kids/13-ways-to-raise-caring-and-compassionate-child.html

Sutton, J., PhD. (2023). Active listening: the art of empathetic conversation. PositivePsychology.com. https://positivepsychology.com/active-listening/

Taming toddler aggression. (n.d.). https://www.
boystownpediatrics.org/knowledge-center/toddler-aggression

Tamm, L. (2021). Why Kids Engage in Power Struggles
(And How to Fix It). The Military Wife and Mom. https://
themilitarywifeandmom.com/why-kid-engages-power-struggles/

Temper tantrums in toddlers: How to keep the peace.
(2022, October 7). Mayo Clinic. https://www.mayoclinic.
org/healthy-lifestyle/infant-and-toddler-health/
in-depth/tantrum/art-20047845

The 5R's of consequences. (2021, November 19).
INCLUDEnyc. https://includenyc.org/help-center/
resources/the-5rs-of-consequences/#:~:text=Defining%20
the%205Rs&text=Reasonable%3A%20
The%20consequence%2C%20like%20a,or%20
consequence%20to%20ensure%20understanding.

The Development and Socialization of aggression
during the first five years of life | Encyclopedia on
Early Childhood Development. (2022, December 1).
Encyclopedia on Early Childhood Development. https://
www.child-encyclopedia.com/aggression/according-experts/
development-physical-aggression-early-childhood-adulthood

Thetherapistparent. (2020, August 6). Recognising our
Triggers and Avoiding Power Struggles. The Therapist
Parent. https://www.thetherapistparent.com/post/
recognising-our-triggers-and-avoiding-power-struggles

Vengrow, B. G. (2022). No, Moms: It's Not Selfish
to Make Yourself a Priority. Parents. https://www.
parents.com/parenting/moms/healthy-mom/
self-care-for-moms-why-its-important-to-make-it-a-priority/

Walt, R. (2020). Raising Kinds Kids: How To Encourage Empathy, Inclusion, and Compassion. Nurture and Thrive. https://nurtureandthriveblog.com/raising-kind-kids/

What every child needs. (n.d.). Children's Hospital Colorado. https://www.childrenscolorado.org/conditions-and-advice/parenting/parenting-articles/what-children-need/

Why spend one-on-one time with your child. (2019, February 14). First Five Years. https://www.firstfiveyears.org.au/child-development/why-spend-oneonone-time-with-your-child

Wilborn, A. L. (2016, August 20). The Secrets to Happiness: Lessons from a Toddler. Tiny Buddha. https://tinybuddha.com/blog/secrets-happiness-lessons-from-a-toddler/

Yanek, D. (2017a, March 28). Toddler Hell on Earth: How I conquered my kid's tantrums at the doctor's office.Healthline. https://www.healthline.com/health/parenting-toddlers-how-i-conquered-the-doctors-office-tantrums

Yanek, D. (2017b, March 28). Toddler Hell on Earth: How I conquered my kid's tantrums at the doctor's office. Healthline. https://www.healthline.com/health/parenting-toddlers-how-i-conquered-the-doctors-office-tantrums#Reworking-the-doctors-visit-strategy

Printed in Great Britain
by Amazon

40275300R00086